D1250923

Ten Great Educators of Modern Japan

Ten Great
Educators of
Modern Japan

A Japanese Perspective

Compiled and Edited by
Benjamin C. Duke

Foreword by
Edwin O. Reischauer

UNIVERSITY OF TOKYO PRESS

GALLAUDET UNIVERSITY LIBRARY
WASHINGTON, D.C. 20002

For bibliographic reasons, the names of the authors of chapters in this book are given in western order, with family names last: Benjamin C. Duke, Kiyoko Takeda Cho. All other Japanese names are given in customary order, with family name followed by personal name.

Translation of this volume was supported by a grant-in-aid from the Ministry of Education, Science and Culture, Japan.

©1989 University of Tokyo Press
ISBN 4-13-057017-X
ISBN 0-86008-442-6

Printed in Japan

No part of this publication may be translated into other languages, reproduced, or utilized in any form or by any means, electronic or mechanical, including photocopying, recording, and microcopying, or by any information storage and retrieval system, without permission in writing from the publisher.

370.952
T4
1989

Dedicated to the memory of

Yuasa Hachiro, President, International Christian University,
Hidaka Daishiro, Dean, Graduate School of Education, International
  Christian University, and
Nishimoto Mitoji, Chairman, Division of Education, International
  Christian University;

Three great Japanese educators who personally influenced my life
  so profoundly.

038581

033581

Contents

Foreword

Japan's rise during the past century and a half from being an isolated, feudal, preindustrial nation on the periphery of world civilization to being the second greatest industrial power on the front edge of world culture is one of the most significant historical developments of modern times. All knowledgeable students of Japan would agree in listing education high among the reasons for this outstanding achievement. Japan's virtually universal literacy, its high levels of school attendance all the way through university, and its ability to impart through formal education great quantities of information, particularly in such fields as mathematics, are world-renowned. This main line of Japanese education seems to have resulted from the careful grafting of Occidental scientific information and patterns of education onto a vigorous trunk of Confucian respect and eagerness for education. This was achieved by wise political leaders, who set the goals, and by a mass of diligent bureaucrats and devoted teachers, who implemented the plans. Their success was great, but, conforming as they did to established policies, they individually remained relatively faceless, as so much of Japanese leadership tends to be.

Despite its solid achievements, this main line of Japanese education had some serious drawbacks. The men and women who sought to correct these weaknesses were, of course, strong individualists who stood out more clearly than their conformist compatriots. It is ten leaders of this type who are singled out for detailed consideration in this book.

The ten are a diverse lot in their careers, personalities, and

ideas. They start with Fukuzawa Yukichi, who differed from the
government educators largely in that he anticipated them and
led the way both in his tremendously popular writings and in
his founding in 1868 of a school which grew into Keio University.
The second, Mori Arinori, was an extremely dynamic and innovative Minister of Education, until his assassination in 1889
at the age of 42. The last, Munakata Seiya, was noted as a backer
of the Japan Teachers' Union in its prolonged fight with the
Ministry of Education for control of the schools and as an opponent of the government's foreign policies.

Most of the rest, including Naruse Jinzo, Uchimura Kanzo,
Tsuda Ume, Nitobe Inazo, and Nambara Shigeru, were ardent
Christians, who drew heavily from American Protestantism for
their educational concepts. They all stressed the development
through education of a sense of individual responsibility and
worth, striving to counteract the tendency of Japanese education to produce uniformity and placid merging into the group,
which are recognized today as being among the greatest weaknesses of Japanese education. Most of the ten were strong supporters of equal educational opportunities for women, another
area of weakness in prewar Japanese education, and three of
them, Naruse, Tsuda, and Nitobe, were founders of women's
universities.

The ten selected in this book were indeed all great educators
in one way or another, helping to correct some of the imperfec-
tions of Japanese education in their time and enriching it immensely. The question remains, however, whether they were
great educators in an international context. All innovators in
education, of course, are reacting to the conditions of the time
and place they know. Because of the similarities among the countries of the West, educational reforms devised in response to
conditions in one country might well be relevant to others, thus
giving the innovator an international standing. In Japan, these
ten were dealing with education in a country that had a very
different historical background and recent national experience
from the countries of the West. The abolition of class distinctions
in education, the emphasis on the importance of the individual,
and the winning of equal educational rights for women were
great and daring steps for Japan but were scarcely new to the

western world. Some of them became confirmed internation-
alists and even pacifists, but most of them retained a strong nationalistic bent and an insistence on the uniqueness of Japanese
culture, which is still one of Japan's greatest flaws today. Fukuzawa became a vociferous imperialist in his later years, and
Shimonaka Yosaburo, an open supporter of Japan's military
aggression in the 1930s.

For the Japan of their time, the ten were important innovators both in education and in other fields. Their careers and
thoughts afford fascinating insights into Japan in their day. Just
because they reflect so clearly the Japan in which they lived,
they cannot be considered educators of worldwide significance.
Japan was just too different from the outside world at that time.
But the times have changed, and conditions in Japan have become much more like those in the other industrialized democra-
cies. Japan and the rest of the world have also become much
more interdependent. Important educators of the years ahead
in Japan may very well prove to be innovators of worldwide
importance.

Cambridge, Massachusetts   EDWIN O. REISCHAUER
August 1989

Preface

This book is an outgrowth of experiences that began in 1959 when
I became an instructor at the International Christian University
in Tokyo. I had just completed the doctorate program at Pennsylvania State University and was searching for a post within
the American educational world. The acceptance of the invitation to teach at a very new university in Japan was intended
merely as a short-term option until a more permanent post in
the United States could be secured.

Contrary to expectations, I slowly and inexorably became
engrossed in the Japanese educational world. This process involved teaching responsibilities in the undergraduate Division
of Education, and a three-year term as chairman of the Graduate
School Division of Education. It also included invaluable experiences as a parent of three children, Susan Noriko, Kimiko Anne,
and Christopher Kenji (now university students) as they progressed through the local Japanese public schools.

What was originally intended as a three-year terminal contract extended into a thirty-year career in Japan, interrupted
only by three years at the University of London completing a
British doctorate. During this thirty-year span, I encountered
in various ways the thoughts and writings of earlier Japanese
educators. Indeed, many of my senior Japanese colleagues at
the university had known intimately several of the most distinguished Japanese educators of the early decades of the 1900s,
and spoke about them with great admiration. Learning more
about these figures, I realized that they were not ordinary teachers. I ultimately concluded that they ranked among the world's

great educators. The inspiration for this book emerged from that realization.

It was natural for me to initially ask my senior colleague, Dr. Kiyoko Takeda Cho, for her reaction to the plan for this book. She enthusiastically encouraged me to proceed, thereby becoming one of the three key individuals who made this book possible. Dr. Cho herself qualifies as a great educator from Japan. However, an early decision was made to exclude living individuals from the book. Dr. Cho graciously agreed to write the chapters on Uchimura Kanzo and Nitobe Inazo, as an authority on both. In addition, she recommended four other authors who joined the project in part because Dr. Cho was participating. Her role was invaluable in the initial stages.

The second individual who was indispensable as well as indefatigable was my graduate assistant, Kazutaka Yamaguchi, currently professor and chairman of the Education Faculty at Saitama National University. Professor Yamaguchi handled the day-to-day details in the compilation of the material. He also undertook the taxing task of providing the initial rough translation of the eight chapters originally written in Japanese. Not only am I grateful for his essential contribution to this publication, but I have also come to respect him as a very fine scholar in the discipline of education. I wish him well in his career.

Finally, I would be derelict if I did not recognize the enormous contribution of my wife, June, who typed the manuscript and its various revisions. She has gone far beyond the call of wifely support, having already typed two Ph.D. theses and their many revisions, two full-length books, and many professional articles. Without her cooperation and understanding, it is unlikely that many of those works would have reached the final stage of publication in an acceptable form.

Tokyo   BENJAMIN C. DUKE
June 1989

Ten Great Educators of Modern Japan

Introduction

Within the international forum of education, the great educators who are recognized as having made outstanding contributions in the field of education are primarily European or American. Among this distinguished group are such illustrious figures as Pestalozzi, Froebel, Herbart, Spencer, and Dewey. From any perspective, they and others like them deserve their exalted place in the history of education as prolific sources of innovative ideas that have withstood the test of time. They will for all times be recognized across national borders, continents, and oceans as truly great educators.

Are there not great educators in Asia, as well, who have made major contributions to the field of education? Assuredly there are, but unfortunately they are for the most part virtually unknown beyond their own borders. Of the very few great educators from this part of the world who are fairly well known, at least in international academic circles, most have been introduced through analyses made by western scholars.

The project of which this volume is the result was designed to search for and identify great educators in Japan—a nation that has developed the most advanced education system in Asia, attaining a mass educational standard surpassed by none in the world—and to make known their contributions to an international audience. Moreover, to avoid western predilections, a Japanese perspective was followed throughout. The determination of who should be classified as a great Japanese educator was made by contemporary Japanese scholars of intellectual history, and the educational contributions made by each of the selected educators were analyzed by Japanese scholars to obtain a wholly Japanese perspective. Only the concept for the study originated with a non-Japanese, the editor, whose aim was providing not only biographies of a number of outstanding Japanese educators but also the opportunity to learn how contemporary Japanese scholars perceive their predecessors.

In order to achieve this goal, forty recognized scholars in the general discipline of education were asked to list five (deceased) persons whom they believed made the greatest contributions to Japanese education since the Meiji Restoration of 1868. The names were then arranged according to frequency. Among the top dozen, ten were selected for this study as "great educators from Japan."

The next step was carried out in consultation with several distinguished Japanese scholars. Based on their recommendations, a recognized authority on each of the ten chosen figures was invited to prepare an essay on the life and contributions of that educator. Except for the two essays by Kiyoko Takeda Cho, which were written in English, these chapters were translated into English by a Japanese translator and rendered into native English by the editor.

Reading the essays, a non-Japanese can readily appreciate the fact that there are indeed great educators from Japan. These individuals have made major contributions to Japanese education during the past century, often under extenuating circumstances unimaginable to great Western educators such as Herbart and Dewey. One cannot help but conjecture whether the great John Dewey, who dominated the international arena of education in the 1920s and 1930s, would have been able to develop his progressive educational thought had he experienced the trials and tribulations of an educational reformer in Japan during the same period.

Certain common characteristics in the thoughts of the great Japanese educators exhibit a remarkable similarity with those of the great educators in the West. Foremost is the progressive nature of their ideas. All were seeking fairly radical reforms, in one way or another, in the existing social order through education. All promoted innovative concepts in Japanese education that, however enlightened, were not acceptable to those with the decision-making power. Most of the great educators in both the East and the West can accordingly be joined together as progressives.

Among the Japanese progressives, there are also certain distinct characteristics that, although not common to them all, are nevertheless prevalent enough for our consideration. Historically, the first vital factor was the influence Christianity exerted on the great educators of Japan. Five of the ten figures in this study were themselves deeply influenced by religious convictions. One, Uchimura Kanzo, was himself the founder of the unique "non-church" (*mukyokai*) movement in Japan, which remains one of the principal Christian influences in the country. Another, Naruse Jinzo, an ordained minister, encouraged students in his new Japan Women's University to follow the teachings of Christ. Tsuda Ume opened her famous school for girls with Bible reading and prayer. And Nitobe Inazo was, along with Uchimura, an original member of the famous Sapporo Band, described as one of the mainstreams of Christianity in Meiji Japan. Finally, Nambara Shigeru, under the influence of Nitobe and particularly of Uchimura, became a convert to Christianity as a young man, eventually becoming the first Christian president of the prestigious University of Tokyo.

The father of modern Japanese education, Mori Arinori, was not among the great educators of Japan who were baptized Christians, but he was deeply influenced by Christianity. Exposed to the rigors of a small Christian sect for over a year in America while still a teenager, he felt the influence of daily prayer and worship in which all residents of the community participated. In fact, one of the reasons for his assassination by a fanatical nationalist was the suspicion that Mori was a Christian who, as Minister of Education, would eliminate traditional Shinto customs in his reformation of Japanese education.

Considering the fact that only a minute number of Japanese were Christians at the turn of the century, the strong influence of Christianity on many leading academic figures of the period is impressive. It is more understandable in the context of another distinct feature in the lives of the earlier Japanese who achieved fame for their progressive thought. American culture (and thus its Christian traditions) played a prominent role in the lives of a significant number of outstanding Japanese educators. Although an ocean away, at the turn of the century the United States beckoned to many a Japanese progressive as a mecca of new ideas for the future development of Japan.

Even to those destined for greatness but devoid of Christian convictions, such as Fukuzawa Yukichi and Sawayanagi Masataro, American culture represented an irresistible attraction. For example, the famous story concerning Fukuzawa—who, after diligently studying the Dutch language from the very earliest westerners allowed into Japan, discovered that he had to begin anew with English, since the most recent foreigners in Yokohama, the Americans, did not speak Dutch—is one of the more revealing anecdotes in modern Japan. Many others joined Fukuzawa in studying the foreign language of English, subsequently finding their way to the United States for formal study or otherwise to learn western ways. Sawayanagi falls within a later group who became attracted to the modern concepts of American progressive education rather than American Christianity. Few Americans to this day are aware of the significant influence their society exerted on many of Japan's early educators.

Another thread that runs through the lives of those who lived in the earlier period of this past one hundred years involves the education of young women. Three of the ten Japanese in this study were instrumental in founding the three most influential universities for women in Japan today: Japan Women's University, Tokyo Women's Christian University, and Tsuda College. In addition, Sawayanagi Masataro was the first president of a national university to accept women into that hallowed preserve for men, setting off quite a stir in educational circles. Many others wrote positively about the subject.

Women's education was largely ignored by the government in those days. Consequently the earlier subjects of our study turned overwhelmingly to private institutions to provide higher education for young women, which was not offered in the public sector, since Sawayanagi's precedent was not followed by other national universities until much later. The influence of Christianity in this endeavor played a critical role not only in the founding of institutions for higher education for women but also in the proliferation of secondary mission schools to prepare girls for advanced education in Christian-related colleges. Thus there was a close relationship between Christianity and education for women in prewar Japan.

A prominent theme inextricably related to those already mentioned running throughout the lives of the earlier great Japanese educators was the struggle between the individual and the society or the state. In the highly homogeneous society that existed in Japan, an inevitable conflict arose between those who were different—that is, the progressive—and the rest. A theocratic state made every effort to sustain a Confucian relationship between the rulers and those they ruled. Conforming to the traditional social patterns was expected of all.

Those who deviated from the social norms, including many of those in this study, experienced anguish in an attempt to establish their true identity. To follow tradition was to reflect the indigenous Japanese roots exemplified by the Imperial Family. To think and act differently from the mainstream exemplified to a certain degree alien or foreign characteristics. The internal ordeal experienced by most early Japanese reformers was not only a test of their identity as Japanese but also a challenge to somehow synthesize or fuse the radically different ideas from the West that attracted them with the traditional Japanese customs of behavior and thought that surrounded them.

The uniqueness of the encounter between Japanese and western traditions in prewar Japan arose from the nature of the outside influences. Although certain European societies with their long-established imperial families and sacred social traditions, including official state religions, attracted more than a few Japanese, it was the radically different social and political developments of the new world of North America that appealed to many of the more progressive Japanese. It was the unlikely vision of the American frontier society thrusting off its European aristocratic roots that attracted the early Japanese reformers.

The revolutionary American people, who not only worshiped at the altar of a Christian god but also glorified the individual, appealed to the likes of the impatient Mori, who designed Japan's modern national school system after serving as Japan's top diplomat in Washington for three years. It called to men like the gentle Nitobe Inazo to study at the fledgling American colleges breaking from their European antecedents with new forms of studies, providing him in turn with an American wife, appropriately of the Quaker persuasion. And it attracted the quixotic Uchimura, who found the stark realities of the new so-called Christian society, with its frontier violence, in sharp contrast with the orderly non-Christian Japanese society, where few found it necessary to lock their doors upon retiring at night.

It was this unusual encounter of the Japanese reformers with the most revolutionary form of Western thought and Christian beliefs, concerning the individual and the state and the individual and God, that greatly affected those Japanese who experienced it firsthand, as did many whose lives are told in this book. How to reconcile the individual freedoms and liberties of a frontier society, where government is fragile at best, with a traditional society, where the individual is subordinated to the state and the Imperial Family, exemplified their ordeal. The mercurial thinker Uchimura united in his mind the East and West with his unique concept of his "two *J*'s." He proclaimed that he loved two *J*'s, Jesus and Japan, and that "I do not know which I love more, Jesus or Japan." It was his forthright way of defining a Japanese Christian who accepted western Christianity without sacrificing his cultural heritage. Even then he found himself an outcast from the mainstream when he refused to bow at school, according to Japanese custom, in obeisance before the Imperial Rescript, a symbol of the state.

Nitobe Inazo achieved international acclaim as the author of the classic work originally written in English on Japanese society, *Bushido: The Soul of a Nation*. Identifying the roots of modern Japan's success as *bushido* ("the way of the warrior") developed from a "samurai society," he attempted to unite East and West by grafting Christianity onto a *bushido* trunk. Accordingly, he quite fittingly envisioned himself as a bridge over the Pacific Ocean.

This combination of American individualism and Protestant Christianity thriving in an atmosphere of religious freedom proved alluring to many of our early great educators. These were truly individualists themselves or they would never have ventured to the great unknown of North America. The young Tsuda Ume, setting sail across the vast Pacific Ocean at the tender age of seven without her parents to experience a Christian environment both at home and at school, epitomizes the adventurous spirit of these future reformers. It was the relative individual freedoms of Protestant Christianity, which opened its arms to all with few demands and restrictions, that beckoned across the great ocean divide to reform-minded Japanese.

The application of Christian principles to education, then, became a popular theme for many Japanese progressives. Christianity had prospered and spread through the West and elsewhere by harnessing education as an instrument of evangelism. Indeed, early American schools taught reading in the context of preparation for Bible reading, a necessary step for salvation in the Protestant tradition. The Christian had to be able to read the scriptures in order to understand and abide by God's word. Thus, education for all Christians was a fundamental concept of early American education.

Many Japanese progressives who studied in America became infected with this Protestant approach to education in which all human beings were equal before their Maker and the individual alone was responsible for his religious convictions and the consequences thereof. Returning to Japan, they became involved in Christian, mainly Protestant, education. This was the basis for their involvement in Christian education for girls in a land where educational provisions for young women were greatly restricted and career opportunities few.

Tsuda Ume, even as a child studying in America, underwent the inevitable struggle to remain Japanese while experiencing the new American lifestyle and the individual freedoms of a Christian home. She wrote her parents that Japan should not imitate foreign countries, with one critical exception: Japanese should become Christians. Such were the trials and tribulations of the future great Japanese educators, some even in childhood, as they tried to synthesize traditional Japanese culture with the radical western ideas emanating primarily from America.

Historically the subjects of this study can be divided rather conveniently between those great educators whose basic mode of thought was formed in the years well before the short-lived period of history known as Taisho Democracy, immediately after World War I, and those who came into prominence during or after that epochal period which sparked an intellectual awakening. Those in the earlier period were deeply influenced by American culture and, in an impressive number of cases, by Christianity, as described above. Those who lived during or after the early 1920s were deeply influenced by the new ideological attraction of socialism and/or progressive education.

Sawayanagi Masataro, nearing the end of his illustrious career, represents in this period a truly unusual reformer who earlier came through the rigid confines of the highest professional post of Vice-Minister in the Ministry of Education, followed by the presidency of several prominent mainline national universities. Yet, he established the progressive and private Seijo School, introducing into Japan the most radical concepts of progressive education, such as the Dalton Plan. Simultaneously, Shimonaka Yosaburo, later to be a most successful businessman, launched the antecedents of Japan's prewar left-wing anti-government teacher's movement. Munakata Seiya was to become the postwar ideologist for the same movement as it resurfaced during the postwar American Occupation and pitted itself against the government, a policy which continues to this day.

Once again, we witness, after World War I and the great period of Taisho Democracy, new Western influences. In this instance it is, first of all, socialism motivated by the Russian communist revolution that provided one spark for progressive ideas. Christian influences remained strong among those Japanese affected accordingly, but even in the West and particularly the United States, Christian influence in education gradually waned as the essentially nonreligious movement of John Dewey's progressive education swept through American schools, providing another spark to fire the Japanese reformers of this era.

The initial relationship between American progressive education and early Russian communist education was peculiar and short-lived. It is true that John Dewey was emulated by some Russian revolutionaries upon his visit to the USSR in the 1920s—as he was on the occasion of his visit to Japan to attend the funeral of Naruse Jinzo. It was in part this unusual relationship between Russian communist revolutionaries and American progressive educators, such as John Dewey, that sparked increased internal interest in the reforms of Japanese education.

Within this vibrant international environment, Shimonaka Yosaburo comes onstage from a destitute childhood representing a different type of Japanese progressive who did not go abroad for study or find Christianity attractive. Rather, through day-to-day experiences in a rigidly controlled, standardized curriculum heavily dominated by morals education with the Imperial system at the center, he began to question the prevailing educational practices. Motivated by the new socialist movements spreading through Europe and the radical educational ideas emanating from North America, this ideologically oriented progressive took the lead in demanding educational reform. Not a Leninist, though a champion of solidarity between teachers and workers and the concept of teachers as laborers, Shimonaka was instrumental in the formation of a left-wing teachers' movement. This took root long before the American Occupation of 1945, which encouraged a teachers' movement independent of government control, culminating in the organization of the giant Japan Teachers' Union.

The theoretical basis for a teachers' union independent of government control was later formalized by such spokesmen as Munakata Seiya, based at the education faculty of the University of Tokyo. Reflecting the age-old theme of the individual versus the state, the new progressive ideologues based their reform demands on the foundation of democratic socialism and the rights of the people versus those of the state. The issue for the modern progressives was simply who should control education in place of the state.

The thread that weaves through many of the proposals by the reformers of this period is their deep concern for the intrinsic value of the human being, reminiscent of an earlier period when Christian influence was strong among many reformers. In both cases they were humanists dissatisfied with an education system under government control that resulted in uniformity and standardization. Borne by the political winds of the 1930s, a heavy concentration of nationalism further reduced the teachers' opportunity to recognize individualism and nourish creativity. The schools of pre-World War II Japan, both before and after the Taisho Democracy period of the 1920s, were prime targets for the reformers from this perspective.

When Shimonaka first championed an independent organization of teachers in the 1920s, the state, falling under militarist
control, reacted sharply to any threat to military supremacy over
what was to be taught in the school and who was to teach it.
Thus began the near total suppression of those who held views
opposite to those of the dominant ultra-nationalists—i.e., suppression of progressives by conservatives, the left by the right.

In the wake of World War II, Americans once again played
a prominent role in Japanese affairs by initially recognizing and
encouraging progressives like Munakata to resume their movements independent of governmental control. With the great
surge of postwar communism in various parts of the world, inevitably some Japanese progressives such as Munakata were
caught up in the resulting euphoria, much to the consternation
of American Occupation leaders, who viewed an apolitical teachers' union and a locally elected school board system as the grass-
roots foundation of a democratic society.

The great left-wing movements during the American Occupation period forged unlikely alliances between different types of
reformers, including left-wing activists such as Munakata, American civilian reformers in the Education Mission to Japan (which
developed the great democratic reforms of postwar Japanese
education), and ideologically moderate but progressive scholars
like the great Nambara Shigeru, president of the University of
Tokyo and a member of the Japanese committee to work with
the American mission in formulating the reforms. All three sides
agreed that state control of education should be sharply curtailed
and the development of the individual given primary concern.
They diverged in their approach to achieving this aim, with
progressives like Munakata forming close links with organizations
under the strong influence of the burgeoning socialist and communist parties of postwar Japan. Other reformers, such as Nambara, viewed educational change essentially from what they
considered a non-ideological perspective, although it was couched
in democratic terminology.

This great post–World War II confrontation over the role and
authority of the state and the individual in the determination
and direction of Japanese education brings us to the end of the
lives of the great educators selected for this study, to the deaths

of Munakata, the professor of educational administration at the University of Tokyo, and Nambara, ironically the chief administrator of the same university. But the basic issues generated by these two great educators and their predecessors, such as Shimonaka in the 1920s, continue as unresolved problems of contemporary Japanese education. The famous Ienaga textbook cases running through the courts for years from the 1960s through the 1980s is a continuation of the question addressed by several of our more recent great educators.[1] Although the immediate issue concerns who should interpret Japanese history for social-studies textbooks, the fundamental question in dispute is essentially the older problem of who should control Japanese education.

Also of considerable interest in these essays, in addition to the lives and thought of the great educators themselves, are the attitudes of contemporary scholars of Japanese education toward their predecessors. The very fact that they chose mainly Christians from the earlier period and ideologically motivated progressives from the latter, divided by the Taisho era, reveals in itself how these scholars analyze Japanese prewar history of the modern era. Of equal importance is their attitudes toward those great educators who lived into the period of Japanese aggression of the 1930s and 1940s. Can a Japanese who condoned or embraced Japanese aggression justifiably be considered a great educator today? If so, how can that be defended when Japanese militarism provoked unspeakable brutalities and inflicted hardships on neighboring countries?

The essay on Shimonaka, and to a lesser extent the one on Munakata, broaches this delicate subject. Shimonaka stands out, since he was purged by American military authorities for his ultranationalism during the war. Even so, most educational scholars today list him as a great educator who made a major contribution to Japanese education. The combination of his critical role in opposing autocratic government in the early 1920s and his leadership role in anti-war and anti-nuclear movements after the war, apparently provides him with sufficient credentials

---

[1] Historian Ienaga Saburo brought suit against the Ministry of Education, challenging its right to "screen" textbooks for use in the public schools and to force changes in the way recent history is depicted therein.

to be legitimately considered a great educator today, in spite of his "reverse course" in the middle period of his life. The recognition of the positive role of Shimonaka and Munakata in Japanese history by contemporary scholars may also indicate a degree of sympathy and understanding for those liberal Japanese who lived through the years when every facet of the society was carried along by an irreversible tide of expansionism under the rigid control of the militarists.

The essay on an earlier figure, Fukuzawa Yukichi, provides a unique balance to the others in that the author, a recognized authority on Fukuzawa, assumes a critical stance toward one of Japan's most respected educators. As the writer notes, "Indeed, of the educators included in this study, Fukuzawa is probably the most widely recognized and popular among the Japanese people." His magnum opus *The Encouragement of Learning* (*Gakumon no Susume*) is regarded to this day as one of the greatest contributions to educational literature produced by any Japanese liberal thinker. At the same time, however, this famous individual, founder of the progressive Keio University, supported Japanese expansion in Asia long before World War II. The discrepancies between what Fukuzawa wrote in his several classics of liberal thought in an earlier period and what he advocated in reality and in his other works of a later era are significant and should be recognized as such, according to this contemporary scholar.

What can we learn from these great educators of Japan? Current issues in Japanese education, for example, can be better understood in the light of historical parallels, particularly through writings of their own great educators. For example, the 1980s have been notable for the widespread criticism of the schools. Government commissions have embarked on official investigations of the educational system in order to develop the "sweeping reforms" called for by the prime minister. The Report of the Interim Council for Educational Reform of June 1985, published by the government of Japan, states that the "principle of putting emphasis on individuality is the fundamental principle which is implied in all other concepts." Later reports also confirm this emphasis.

History is indeed repeating itself. For the past one hundred years outstanding Japanese educators have been calling for greater emphasis on the individual in the schools. During the Occupation of Japan, the Americans joined the cause by making certain that the concept was included in the 1947 Fundamental Law of Education. The preamble proclaims that "we shall esteem individual dignity," and Article I, "Aims of Education," that "education shall aim at the full development of personality . . . striving for the rearing of people . . . who esteem individual value." The call for individuality as the twentieth century closes now comes from a government commission itself. The times have changed; the players have become reversed; but the message remains the same.

If we are to learn anything of future significance from the history and legacy of the great Japanese educators of the past, it may be that the current reforms "putting emphasis on individuality" may still be too radical for the prevailing customs of Japanese society. Even though a government organ directly responsible to the prime minister's office has produced reform proposals reminiscent of those made by outstanding educators of a former period, it seems likely that many more years may elapse before these recurring themes advance beyond the proposal stage. Nevertheless, the contemporary efforts to reform Japanese education for the twenty-first century based on individuality demonstrate just how radical and how far ahead of their times were Japan's great educators of the past one hundred years who committed themselves to achieving the same goal.

Fukuzawa Yukichi in 1887, at the peak of his career.

Fukuzawa Yukichi

[1834–1901]

Jyunosuke Yasukawa

In 1984, the picture of Fukuzawa Yukichi first appeared on the ¥10,000 bank note of the Japanese currency. It was a symbolic recognition of Fukuzawa's contribution as one of the most outstanding and enlightened figures in the modernization of Japanese society and culture following the Meiji Restoration. He is also very well known as the founder of Keio University, one of the most distinguished of all private universities in the land. Indeed, of the great educators included in this study, Fukuzawa is probably the most widely recognized and popular among the Japanese people.

At the same time that Fukuzawa's picture first appeared on the bank note, a reader of one of the major Japanese daily newspapers wrote a letter to the editor appealing for the discontinuation of that particular note. The writer complained that the use of the picture on the new Japanese currency demonstrated a total disregard of a "sense of internationalism," since Fukuzawa advocated Japanese expansionism and aggression in Asia. That letter must have been a surprise to many readers, because Fukuzawa's support of Japanese expansion in Asia is not generally known.

Since Japan maintained its independence during the era of Western colonialism in Asia and rapidly modernized through capitalist development while launching aggressive actions against its Asian neighbors, it is understandable that Fukuzawa's role could invite a divided reaction. His contributions to Japanese education can be viewed from two perspectives. On the one hand, his emphasis on the education of a cultivated people could be construed as an effort to increase productivity for the development of a capitalistic economy as Japan endeavored to catch up with the advanced western capitalist economies. On the other hand, Fukuzawa's deep concern for the advancement of education could also be construed as an effort to effectively prepare the nation for the overseas aggression that led to such fanatical acts as the Rape of Nanking, China, in 1937. Consequently the analysis of Fukuzawa's contribution to Japanese education will be considered from the perspective of this dual nature of modern Japanese history.

Fukuzawa Yukichi was born the fifth son of a lesser samurai family of the Nakatsu clan at their residence in Osaka, the commercial center second only to Edo (now Tokyo). He actually grew up, however, with his mother and siblings in the town of Nakatsu, in Kyushu, since Fukuzawa's father died when the boy was only two years old. Compared with his father's highly restricted and regulated life as a lower-level samurai, Fukuzawa's adolescence was marked with promise and hope in the future as the feudal patterns of the society were slowly undergoing change after so many years of isolation from the outside world.

Japan was about to face the most tumultuous era in its long history. The nation was soon to be opened to the world as the American Commodore Matthew C. Perry sailed his famous fleet of "black ships" off the shore of Uraga in 1853. This bold defiance of Japan's long-standing policy of seclusion compelled the feudal government to face up to the new realities in international relations. Fukuzawa was only eighteen years old at this time.

The total isolation of Japan had already been slightly breached by the presence of a small Dutch contingent in Nagasaki at the southern tip of Kyushu, the only opening to the outside world before the coming of Commodore Perry. A few select boys were allowed to study Western science from Dutch teachers through the medium of the Dutch language. Fukuzawa was one of the few chosen to have this early experience of a year of things western. All this was taking place during the closing days of the Tokugawa period.

Fukuzawa moved to Osaka to enter Teki Juku, the most famous private school teaching *rangaku* ("Dutch studies"), where

Fukuzawa in 1862, while visiting Paris.

A diplomatic mission to the United States, in Washington, D.C., in 1867. Fukuzawa is at the far right.

In riding attire, 1874.

Fukuzawa in 1900, shortly before his death.

this western learning was being passed on by those Japanese who had studied with the Dutch in Kyushu. Fukuzawa took the further study of western science seriously enough to be selected the leader of the student body. Later, in 1858, when the U.S.–Japan Treaty of Friendship was signed, he was instructed to open up his own small school teaching *rangaku* to members of the Nakatsu clan at their residence in Edo. That early school turned out to be the beginning of the distinguished Keio University of today.

Shortly thereafter the Japanese government cautiously opened the nearby port of Yokohama to foreign trade. Fukuzawa traveled to the new facility, only to realize that his Dutch was useless. The new traders used English. Fukuzawa decided there and then that he had to learn English if he were ever going to help his country face the enormous challenge confronting it in its new opening to the world.

In 1860, Fukuzawa offered his services to the Shogunate military government as an assistant on the first ship to make an official visit to the United States. The party was simply overwhelmed by western civilization and the unique social system of the United States. The young Fukuzawa returned to Japan dazzled with what he had seen in America.

Fukuzawa was then employed by the Tokugawa government as a translator of diplomatic documents. This work, coupled with his earlier visit to the United States, set him to ponder the future of his country in international affairs. At the same time his position made it possible for him to marry into a higher-ranked samurai family of the same clan. All of these developments, he realized, came about as a result of his education, a fact he pointed out often in later life.

At the end of his first year of marriage, Fukuzawa was appointed an official staff member of a governmental mission to the West. The trip took about one year—five months on the high seas and the remainder visiting six European countries. In the process he was able to collect many foreign books. Fukuzawa was thus able to broaden his intellectual horizons, both through his travel and through the many books he brought back with him. Above all he witnessed for the first time the miserable conditions of the native people living under western colonialism during stopovers in British Ceylon and Hong Kong. He realized that advanced western countries ruled the poor nations of Asia under the principal of "might is right."

"First of all, it is urgent that our people enrich and strengthen our country. The foundation must be an educated citizenry." This statement, in a letter from London to a member of his clan, was the first in his correspondence referring to the future of Japan. It clearly revealed his way of thinking, which remained fundamental to him throughout his life. He insisted on equality in international relationships on the basis of natural law. But "might is right" was constant in his approach to international relations. In his view, the independence of the state was founded on the wealth and military power of the nation. To the young Fukuzawa, living during the fading days of the Tokugawa era, the social system he advocated seemed far from achievable. What he sought was a unified state under the feudalistic Tokugawa Shogunate, the promotion of civilization and enlightenment, and the achievement of wealth and military power by the state.

Further maturing of Fukuzawa's thought would lead him to advocate the concept of strengthening the state through the education of its citizenry. Unfortunately, however, at the very time of his return from his extended visit to various European countries in 1862, the isolationist policies of the feudal Tokugawa Shogunate were approaching their zenith in a final mood of desperation. The military dynasty was drawing to a close. During this period the few students of western learning were simply relegated to a quiet life. Fukuzawa settled down to a contemplative life studying the many books he had collected when traveling abroad and managing his small private school teaching western studies.

However, by 1864, the fervor for isolationism began its inevitable decline, and external pressure forced the government to establish more international contacts. Fukuzawa became a staff member of the Bureau of Translation of the Foreign Department, again offering his services to the government. Fukuzawa was by then obviously growing impatient with his relative inactivity. His mind was bursting with new ideas. For example, at this time he began writing the manuscript for *Seiyo Jijo* (*Conditions in the West*), which later turned out to be one of the great classics of

Japanese modern history, providing one of the first opportunities for the Japanese to gain an introduction to western culture.

Once again Fukuzawa volunteered to join a government mission to the United States, scheduled for 1867, with the assignment of purchasing a modern warship. Fukuzawa characteristically used the opportunity to collect many foreign books. However, during the trip he came into conflict with the leader of the mission. Upon his return to Japan he was confined to his home—in effect, placed under house arrest. The incident convinced him that political affairs were not his forte, and he resolved to devote himself to a life of teaching in his private school and to concentrate on writing.

Several months after he was acquitted of the charges against him stemming from the trip abroad, the Tokugawa government collapsed. Fukuzawa, a loyal subject of the Shogunate who had served on several governmental missions overseas, was further convinced that a political life was not for him. Most of his colleagues chose a similar path. And yet, he was deeply disturbed by the slogans of those who supported the return of Imperial rule under the new emperor Meiji, which appeared at the beginning to be adhering to the old isolationist policies more firmly than ever. "Revere the Emperor! Expel the barbarians [foreigners]!" became the rallying cry of the Imperial forces in their bid to oust the old military government of the Tokugawa family. Fukuzawa did not fully understand the nature of this highly nationalistic movement to overthrow the old regime that he had served. At first he was disillusioned with the new government.

At this time the first edition of *Conditions in the West* had a highly successful debut, selling more than 200,000 copies. Fukuzawa now became very well known throughout Japan. Suddenly he realized that he could support himself quite successfully as a writer and teacher. He came to the realization that the intelligentsia and the middle classes had a definite role to play in Japanese society. He began formulating his opinions in another work called *Gakumon no Susume* (*Encouragement of Learning*), which is now recognized as one of the great classics of the period.

In 1868, ten years after the beginning of his private school, the Imperial army marched triumphantly into Edo, the capital of the Shogunate. Fukuzawa moved his school to a new location within the city and named it Keio Gijuku, after the name of the previous imperial era. Keio was what could be called the first modern private school in Japan to be established independently of both the national government and any clan association. His tuition system for student payment also represented the first of its kind in the land. By 1870 the number of students had increased to over three hundred. The school was again moved— to Mita, in Tokyo—were it remains today as the main campus of Keio University.

When the new Meiji government finally brought local opposition to an end, the new leaders, rather than following the old policy of seclusion, began the search for innovative ways to modernize. Fukuzawa was taken by surprise, since he had expected Imperial rule to be conservative. From that moment onward, Fukuzawa saw his purpose in life from a new perspective. Rather than continuing as simply an intellectual writer interpreting western culture and institutions for Japan, he became an active leader in the new age of enlightenment. A new world for Japan was about to be opened. Fukuzawa became determined to play an active role in it.

An example of the new course of events took place when the government abolished the feudal domain system and replaced it with a system of prefectural governments. Fukuzawa recognized this change as a revolutionary effort to modernize the way Japan was governed. He declared that, accordingly, he wanted "to help establish a great new civilized society in Asia, located far from western countries but inspired by western culture, to cultivate a new enlightened people of Japan."

Based on this declaration, he completed the draft of *Encouragement of Learning*, which had great influence on Japanese education and society. This, coupled with the fame that had resulted from the publication of *Conditions of the West*, established Fukuzawa at the age of thirty-seven as one of the most influential figures in the nation. From that time until his death nearly thirty years later, he played a major role in advising—some would say directing—the new government in Japan in its search for the keys to modernization.

In 1872 the Meiji government issued one of the most important proclamations of modern Japan, the *Gakusei*, outlining the educational ideals for the nation. It marked the beginning of the first national school system. Of the greatest significance, the content of the government's report was remarkably similar to Fukuzawa's *Encouragement of Learning*. Consequently, many observers at the time concluded, half in jest, that although the new Ministry of Education was located at Takebashi, in downtown Tokyo, the Minister of Education was located at Mita (that is, at Keio University). Fukuzawa was thought by many to be the "behind-the-scenes" minister of education.

In *Encouragement of Learning*, Fukuzawa wrote that no man is born destined to be rich or poor; rather, the individual who studies and learns becomes noble and wealthy, while the uneducated become destitute. He argued that education should emphasize the practical: that which serves the needs of the typical Japanese. It should be offered to all, regardless of rank—a revolutionary concept at a time when rank remained an important factor within the society. The book had great appeal to all classes.

In 1875, extending his thought from *Encouragement of Learning*, Fukuzawa published *Bunmeiron no Gairyaku* (*Outline of a Theory of Civilization*), representing another of the great works of the period of early modernization of Japan. In this book Fukuzawa argued that the new government, in opening Japan to the world in its path toward modernization, should not base its developing relations with other nations on the prevailing "laws of international diplomacy." The harsh rule by advanced western capitalistic nations over their defenseless colonies with poorly educated populaces should, he said, serve as a warning to the emerging Meiji government. He concluded that the ability of a country to maintain its independent traditions and culture in the world of the 1870s depended on the level of the culture of the society. The aim of the new Japan was to preserve its sovereignty. The education of its people was the means to achieve it.

The thrust of Fukuzawa's thought concerning the modernization of Japan can be summarized in the following sequence: enlightenment of the people; development of capitalism; preservation of national sovereignty with a strong military and economic foundation. He called for an education that provided wisdom and skills urgently needed by the state. This was certainly not an uncommon view of the day. Most of the leaders of the new government recognized the necessity of the new school system as a prerequisite for the growth of industry and an increase in productivity, as well as the development of a strong military through conscription.

In *Encouragement of Learning*, Fukuzawa anticipated the requirements of the new Japanese government during the era of colonialism dominated by powerful western industrialist countries. Consequently he advocated practical skills for the individual advancement of the ordinary people living in Japan in the 1870s. It was essential, he said, that every Japanese citizen attend school. One of Fukuzawa's favorite themes was the theory that if the individual becomes independent, the nation can preserve its independence. He faced formidable problems in attempting to achieve this aim, since the economic base of the new government was unstable at best during the transition from the old Shogunate to the new Imperial rule. Disarray in the national economy hindered the development of the sense of nationalism so indispensable in the shift from feudalism to Western-style capitalism. He confessed how difficult it was to "enrich the country through education" from the top down—that is, by such means as compulsory education—when the nation was confronted with such enormous social and economic problems.

His *Outline of a Theory of Civilization* was not just a thesis on contemporary problems of modernization. Fukuzawa argued that the preservation of Japanese sovereignty from colonial power was only one problem confronting the nation in the development of its culture. He had another view on the development of history. He began, understandably, with the necessity of striving for national independence, laying aside other matters for the future until this could be assured. Therefore he argued that the nation must not abandon the traditional elements of its society. Even certain feudal concepts, such as Confucian morality or the relationship between the lord and his retainers, should be preserved so as to maintain social cohesiveness in order to attain national independence. This goal, Fukuzawa believed, takes precedence over everything else.

Thus conflicting viewpoints appear in Fukuzawa's writings. For example, he emphasized the independence of the individual as a means of achieving national independence. And yet, in

Encouragement of Learning, his promotion of individual advancement is in the cause of loyalty and patriotism in which the individual lays down his life for his country. In a similar manner, his theory of a social contract stresses the obligation of the citizen to pay his taxes obediently without the right to resist governmental authority, on the assumption that the people already have a social contract with their government protecting their rights under an absolute monarchy.

Fukuzawa's thoughts on education deserve particular attention. In his *Outline of a Theory of Civilization* he wrote that he would gradually make clear in the future the "main purpose of culture." However, the actual course he followed thereafter was contrary to what one could expect. For example, his promotion of such concepts as the heredity of talent, education as a commodity, a pluralistic school system based on wealth, control of textbooks, and segregated education of boys and girls all appear contradictory to his image as one of the foremost enlightened thinkers in modern Japan.

His specific ideas on the education of the masses is a case in point. During the early decades of the Meiji era, the people at large were incapable of realizing the importance of a new national school system to replace the old feudal schools such as those held in temples. At the same time, economic and social conditions made it impossible for the government to build overnight a modern mass school system. The monumental task of establishing a modern school system to produce an educated population—one that could develop a solid economic and social foundation to support a modern school system—faced the new government. The first step in the process was for the national government to enforce compulsory education.

Since a national system of education was implemented from the top down, Japan lagged far behind other nations in treating education as an inherent right of the people. Fukuzawa's thought was no exception to the prevailing viewpoint. He believed that public education should be made compulsory under the authority of the Imperial government. At the same time he advocated education for self-improvement and appealed for a practical education that would result in the realization by the masses of the advantage and utility of being educated.

In contrast to some western school systems of the period, the new Japanese school provided fairly equal educational opportunities for the masses of elementary-school children regardless of social class, although there were extremes ranging from the elite school for members of the Imperial family and ranking aristocrats to the outcast *buraku* schools. In addition, because public middle and higher schools were established, individual advancement leading to social mobility became a reality of the society. These avenues to more and more education for the masses were underlying factors in the great popularity of Fukuzawa's *Encouragement of Learning*. It also laid the basis for the enthusiasm the Japanese people have for education.

Fukuzawa was ambivalent about compulsory education. At first, in the 1870s, he supported it. However, when the Japanese economy became depressed in the mid-1880s, he came to oppose it; a few years later, he opposed a bill enforcing compulsory education of children of the very poor. But following the Sino-Japanese War, which brought a considerable indemnity to the Japanese government and a consequent rapid growth of heavy industry, he became an ardent supporter of compulsory public education. His thoughts concerning compulsory education had a strong economic component.

Fukuzawa's ideas on private education were also somewhat contradictory. Many young scholars studying Fukuzawa, reflecting their expectations, anticipate that because of his own experiences as the founder of a famous private school he would naturally emphasize the "freedom and independence of education." However, in prewar Japan such freedom was not permitted. Fukuzawa's opinion must be seen within the framework of the conditions of the period.

The Meiji government constructed a hierarchical school structure, placing the Imperial universities at the pinnacle. These universities were awarded certain privileges as institutions which primarily prepared an elite group of students for careers in government service. Accordingly their graduates were exempt from military conscription and were not required to sit for national qualifying examinations as teachers or physicians.

Private-school graduates received no such privileges. Nor did their institutions receive governmental support. Rather, in prewar

Japan, private universities came under the control of the government, in a way similar to public institutions. They did not, however, receive public financial support. For example, Fukuzawa opened branches of Keio University in Osaka, Kyoto, and Tokushima in the 1870s. All of them were forced to close within a year, in part for financial reasons. The main campus of the university itself was always facing financial crises during Fukuzawa's lifetime.

In order to accommodate existing conditions, Fukuzawa made certain compromises. For example, when Keio University's unique exemption from required military service of its graduates was abolished by the Military Conscription Act of of 1883, he wrote a letter of petition to the commanding officer of the Japanese army. He agreed to allow officials of the Ministry of Education to give lectures at the university in return for an extension of the exemption. He also requested governmental financial assistance in return for total submission to governmental control.

Fukuzawa's initial ideas about private education were primarily based on the need to reduce governmental expenditures. He felt that private bodies would be more efficient than public bodies from a financial point of view. He also felt that the content of the private-university curriculum would be no different from that of public universities; the only difference would lie in the financial responsibility. The Meiji government followed a similar line of reasoning concerning the differences between public and private universities in its rationale for government control without support.

Fukuzawa initially felt that private-school tuition should not be so low that the children of the very poor could receive higher education. He was concerned that poor people, if educated, could develop into an opposition movement against the government. He knew only too well that the spread of educational opportunities in England had led to a socialist movement among the working classes. Accordingly he advocated secondary and higher education only for the higher classes in order to prevent bright boys from the lower classes from receiving advanced education. He once wrote that one of the most dangerous consequences of education is "the poor with wisdom."

Following this line of thought, Fukuzawa reasoned that talent is inherited and that only the offspring of the better classes of farmers and merchants receive the "genes of talent." In a capitalistic society, education and learning are in a sense commodities to be purchased. Japanese education should be structured so that appropriate education can be purchased by those who can afford it according to wealth and ability: a lower education for the poor and a higher education for the better classes.

Based on these ideas, Fukuzawa concluded that private schools could play a role in the national scheme of education by securing support on a modest scale from the government. In return, private schools would contribute to the maintenance of the social order while contributing to the overall national finances by being more fiscally responsible than the schools administered by the government itself. This represented a reversal of Fukuzawa's former ideals of freedom and originality of the private school. "Sacrifice for patriotism" thus became the founding spirit of Keio University.

Concerning women's education, Fukuzawa expressed his opinion in approximately one hundred essays, including "On Japanese Women," "On the Association of Men and Women," "On Japanese Men," "About Women's Education," and "The New Greater Learning for Women." In all of these publications he repeatedly criticized the widespread practice among high-ranking government officals of supporting mistresses. His strong opposition to this custom, carried over from the feudal period in Japan, was one of the factors in Fukuzawa's reputation as a progressive defender of women's rights at a time when such a position was not popular.

However, from the contemporary perspective of women's rights, his attitude toward women was incongruous. For example, Fukuzawa approved of state-regulated prostitution, which distorted men's attitudes toward sex and women. He also disregarded the root causes of adultery within the upper levels of the society. Apparently he was not advocating the human rights of women when he opposed adultery, but rather the preservation of the dignity of the government, primarily from a diplomatic point of view.

Fukuzawa's concept of women's education reflected the social mores of the period. In "On Japanese Women" he claimed that "a woman should help the man at home" with household work and by taking care of the children. She was destined as her calling to be an obedient, virtuous wife for her husband. He advocated female education separate from that for males in regard to content and academic level, since he believed that females are biologically weaker than males.

Fukuzawa also became well known for his promotion of the "independence of learning." This, too, should be analyzed in the context of the period. His "independence" implied that all those in the field of education, including both teachers and students, should avoid political involvement, such as in the contemporary Freedom and People's Rights Movement. His proposed Academic Affairs Society (Gakujikai) was intended as an apolitical central bureau of educational affairs that would ensure the political neutrality of education.

Yet, at the same time, Fukuzawa supported governmental approval of school textbooks by the Ministry of Education in order to avoid content that would be detrimental to the national policy of strengthening the country. He also supported the Meiji Constitution, which did not include a provision for freedom of learning. When the Imperial Rescript on Education was promulgated, aiming at governmental control of the spiritual values of the people, Fukuzawa did not protest. Although he had written more than a hundred articles on religion, at the time of the lèse-majesté incident in which Uchimura Kanzo, the well-known Christian, was fired from his teaching post for refusing to bow before the Imperial Rescript, Fukuzawa remained silent while the academic world was deeply shaken. And when Minister of Education Mori Arinori enacted the Imperial University Ordinance of 1886, which included provisions for an Imperial university to serve the interest of the state, Fukuzawa welcomed the decision.

The two sides of Fukuzawa on education received attention even before World War II. For example, Okubo Toshikane, one of the most famous scholars in the field of Japanese history of education, wrote that Fukuzawa's understanding of academic freedom of the university was quite different from that in the West. At the same time there were distinguished scholars who praised his writings on freedom and independence of education. During the later years of Fukuzawa's life, his attitudes and opinions underwent an evolutionary change from the earlier idealistic period. In his tenacious concern for national independence through strength, he gradually deviated from his earlier liberal ideas. As the reality of building a strong, independent nation proved increasingly difficult, he became more and more convinced of the need for an absolute monarchy. He also became convinced of the need for Japan to expand its power throughout Asia; otherwise the nation could not maintain its independence at a critical period in history when powerful western countries were carving up neighboring lands into colonial empires.

In the interest of securing national independence, Fukuzawa's thought concerning Japanese internal social and political activities followed a predictable course. For example, in order to maintain domestic social stability, he recognized the need to maintain certain relationships of feudal Japan between the rising class of capitalists and the workers, between landlords and tenant farmers, and between the sovereign and his subjects, His earlier writings, for which he is still widely acclaimed as one of Japan's most enlightened thinkers, advocated the spread of education for social advancement among the downtrodden classes. The international realities of the ensuing era brought about a shift in his attitudes that few contemporary Japanese fully comprehend or appreciate.

Fukuzawa's ideas on religion also underwent an evolutionary swing. His earlier prolific writings on religion urged the cultivation of the people through religious tenets, primarily those of Buddhism. However, in his quest for social stability as a foundation for national strength and solidarity, he became an advocate of the imperial system in his later years. Japanese society was still too immature to be exposed to modern religious thought.

Concerning the rise of capitalism and the industrial revolution, a factor Fukuzawa could not have foreseen in his writings during the mid-1800s, he viewed the rapid industrialization process at the turn of the century in terms of national strength and independence. He admired the great industrial house of Mitsubishi as the epitomization of capitalism at its best. In his view, workers' organizations and rights were subordinated to the modernization and independence of Japan based on the middle classes, the backbone of society. He expressed concern about a socialist or communist movement that could disrupt the social structure as the nation industrialized, provoking an inevitable class struggle between the rich and the poor.

His writings on nationalism are of special interest since they too underwent a transformation as time went by. From his early days he recognized the urgency of maintaining Japan's independence and sovereignty. His advocacy of learning to raise the society's standards in *Encouragement of Learning* inspired a sense of nationalism throughout the land, even though there were strong remnants of feudalistic thought in his writings. His *Outline of a Theory of Civilization*, which inspired a sense of deep patriotism stimulating national integration, was based on the loyal-retainer concept. Combining feudalism, nationalism, and progressivism, Fukuzawa's writings served as a powerful catechism for a nation plunged into the modernization process.

Originally, Fukuzawa was a strong supporter of a national parliament. However, as various political organizations emerged that interpreted the rights and powers of a new parliament from divergent viewpoints, Fukuzawa began to reconsider his earlier position. Political disintegration and social disunity, he feared, could provoke foreign colonial powers to intervene in Japanese domestic affairs. In "Problems of Popular Rights Movements" and "Problems of National Rights," published in 1878, he concluded that a national parliament was premature for the new nation trying to transfer the allegiance of its citizenry from local clans to a new national government. Idealism once again gave way to reality.

Fukuzawa was consequently confronted by the contradictions facing Japan in the great transformation from feudalism to western-type modernism. To secure independence, national strength was essential. This, in turn, had to be based on a solid industrial foundation. Industrialization required a better-educated citizenry. At the same time, education and industrial progress inevitably provoked profound social changes with the rise of a working class that could disturb domestic tranquility. Dissident social and political movements could arise, threatening a breakdown in social cohesion and nationalistic attitudes. This, in turn, could

invite foreign intervention, leading precisely to that which Fukuzawa feared most.

The great contradictions in modernizing societies provoked
much soul-searching for Fukuzawa in his later years. The prominent liberal educator had, in a word, become transformed into
a conservative, nearly irrational nationalist. For example, he
ultimately took a strong stand against Christianity, arguing that
the western religion looked at the world's people as the family
of God, which stood as a major obstacle to the development of
Japan's national feelings and power. His early attitude toward
mass education underwent revision, as disillusionment in the
common people as the motive force for a powerful, independent
nation set in. Searching for a powerful device to unite the people
while strengthening the country both industrially and militarily,
Fukuzawa finally settled on the role of the Emperor. His defense
of the Emperor system, "The Imperial House," was one of his
most significant later writings, demonstrating how far his frustration had carried him from his earlier days, when he had been
free from the constraints of the need to implement his ideas. His
strong support for Japanese aggression in Taiwan, Korea, and
China to build a new order to prevent western aggression exemplified the metamorphosis he underwent.

The image of Fukuzawa among the Japanese that followed
him to death and beyond was not that of an ultranationalist.
Rather, the people looked upon him primarily as one of the
greatest educators who had ever lived. Upon his death in 1901,
fifteen thousand mourners stretched for several miles in the funeral
procession. A former president of Keio University, Koizumi
Shinzo, aptly summed up the feelings of most Japanese people
from all walks of life toward Fukuzawa upon his death:

When Fukuzawa died, he was regarded as one of the most
revered educators of Japan. He was, so to speak, a teacher
to the nation. Shortly after his death, the Lower House of
Parliament passed a resolution expressing condolences: "We
recognize with great respect and admiration the profound
contribution Fukuzawa Yukichi made to Japanese education and to Japan."

Fukuzawa's reputation among contemporary Japanese ranks among the very highest. There can be no doubt that the vast majority of the people see him as one of Japan's "patron saints." Few have any negative feelings toward this most famous figure. His stature was further elevated when the government honored him by choosing him to adorn the new ¥10,000 bank note.

However, an evaluation of Fukuzawa's contributions to Japan should not be based only on his early books, which are still considered classics and have been translated into many languages. Rather, his earlier masterpieces should be compared with his later works, which reveal a less than idealistic attitude toward the realities of international relationships at the turn of this century. When his total output is considered from a purely analytical perspective, two sides to Fukuzawa become apparent.

Among Japanese scholars, the dichotomy in Fukuzawa's thinking is a matter of record. The late historian Hani Goro called him a great thinker who developed a systematic theory of thought. The political scientist Maruyama Masao described him as a man of principle and creativity. The historian Toyama Shigeki claimed that Fukuzawa's frequent conversions did not stem from opportunism but rather from flexibility based on principle.

Another group takes a critical position. For example, the economist Ouchi Hyoe called Fukuzawa a conformist undeserving of the honors that have been bestowed upon him. The scholar and critic Kuga Katsunan claimed Fukuzawa never opposed feudalism and was essentially an arch-conservative. The *Tokyo Daily News*, in announcing Fukuzawa's death, wrote that he did not have philosophic principles.

Such inconsistencies where education was concerned were not confined to Fukuzawa. A number of Japan's leaders, especially those in or near the government, went through such transitions during Japan's period of modernization. Modern Japanese education is still characterized by a double nature: ostensibly heavily influenced by lofty western principles, it in actuality has always been subordinate to the political and economic interests of the state.

It has often been pointed out that the Meiji government accomplished an educational miracle by developing a modern school system in a short period of time in comparison with the growth of western school systems. If numbers of schools and percentages of school attendance are used as the primary criteria for evaluating educational modernization in Japan, then that conclusion is justified. But such achievements were the result of government initiative, which relegated education to the whims of political expediency. Under such conditions it was virtually impossible for a Japanese to develop a universal philosophy of education ahead of his time.

The contributions of Fukuzawa Yukichi must be seen from this historical vantage point, rather than from a western perspective or a contemporary viewpoint. His writings must be viewed from the Japan of the late 1800s, casting off its isolationism, embarking on a historic venture to modernize in order to remain independent during the height of a western colonial expansion that engulfed nearly all backward nations. In this process Fukuzawa made a major contribution in the establishment of a modern school system that strengthened the country—preserving, as he himself so earnestly desired, Japan's sovereignty.

The Life of Fukuzawa Yukichi

1834   Born into a samurai family in Osaka.

1854   Studied the Dutch language and western science at Nagasaki.

1855   Entered a private school, Teki Juku, in Osaka to continue Dutch studies.

1858   Established a private school of Dutch studies in Tokyo.

1859   Began the study of English.

1860   Traveled to the United States with a government mission; upon return, entered full-time government service.

1862   Traveled to Europe with a government mission.

1866   Published *Conditions in the West* (*Seiyo Jijo*).

1867   Traveled to the United States with a naval mission.

1868 Founded Keio Gijuku (forerunner of Keio University) in Tokyo.

1872 Published *Encouragement of Learning (Gakumon no Susume)*.

1873 Participated in the founding of Meirokusha, an academic society of leading intellectuals.

1875 Published *Outline of a Theory of Civilization [Bunmeiron no Gairyaku]*.

1879 Elected Chairman of Tokyo Gakushiin (an academic society).

1882 Published *The Imperial House (Teishitsu Ron) and Moral Education (Tokuiku Ikan)*.

1883 Published *Independence of Learning (Gakumon no Dokuritsu)*.

1898 Suffered a stroke.

1899 Published his autobiography (*Fuku o Jiden*).

1901 Died.

About the Author

Jyunosuke Yasukawa was born in 1935 in Hyogo Prefecture, and graduated from Kobe University's Faculty of Education in 1959. He received the Doctor of Education degree in 1972 from Nagoya University, served as Professor at Saitama University, and is currently Professor at Nagoya University. His publications (in Japanese) include *The Philosophical Structure of Modern Japanese Education: The Educational Thought of Fukuzawa Yukichi* (1970), *An Outline of World Education* (1976), and *The History of Japanese Education* (1985).

Mori Arinori as Ambassador to Washington.

Mori Arinori

[1847–1889]

Terumichi Morikawa

On the morning of February 11, 1889, Minister of Education Mori Arinori was scheduled to attend the promulgation ceremony of the new Imperial Constitution. Dressed in formal attire, he waited for the official carriage to take him to the great event heralded by the government as a monumental stride forward in the modernization of Japan. For Mori, who had carried out unprecedented educational reforms since 1885, it was truly a moment of great historical consequence.

Unannounced, Nishino Buntaro, a former samurai from Yamaguchi Prefecture, called at the Mori home in Tokyo, purportedly on a matter of great urgency. As the secretary received the guest at the entrance, Mori came downstairs. Suddenly the visitor rushed at the unsuspecting Mori, driving a knife into his chest. Mori died the following day at the age of forty-two.

What was intended as a glorious event in the life of the father of the modern Japanese school system turned into a tragedy of state. As Minister of Education, Mori had looked forward to completing his sweeping reforms of education, initiated with the first School Ordinance of 1886, under the new constitution. Although still a young man, he envisioned his remaining proposals as a culmination of the complete transformation of Japanese education.

Curiously, the assassin of one of the greatest educators in Japanese history received considerable sympathy from the public upon his execution for the crime. It was reported that many people shortly thereafter quietly visited his grave. A well-known conservative figure, Kaieda Nobuyoshi, upon learning of the murder, was quoted as saying that the assassination was not totally unanticipated. His reaction was taken as an indication not only of expectation but of tacit approval of the assassin's motives.

Why was Mori assassinated at the very peak of his career? And why did so many Japanese from various walks of life sympathize more with the assassin than with his victim? Even Motoda Nagazane, arch-conservative advisor to the Emperor and leading opponent of educational reform, eventually came around to support Mori. This was significant to Mori, a nationalist who, like Motoda, advocated Imperial duties over new constitutional rights. Still, the widespread opposition to Japan's first Minister of Education and his great reforms of the nation's schools remains something of an enigma.

Mori's attacker revealed his motives in a document later made public. He claimed that Mori deserved to die as just punishment for his disrespectful contempt for the Emperor on the occasion of a recent visit to the Great Shrine at Ise, the hallowed grounds of the supreme shrine of State Shinto. On a school inspection trip around Mie Prefecture, the Minister of Education used the opportunity to visit the shrine. As he stepped into the inner sanctuary he used his cane to raise the screen intended to shield the most sacred objects from public view, violating one of the oldest customs of the ancient faith. It was considered a shameful act of lèse-majesté.

Shinto authorities were already obsessed with fear that Mori, considered a liberal Minister of Education, would oppress Shintoism and its unique role in the schools. Their concern was further aggravated by the general belief that Mori was also a Christian. Such widespread fear among the faithful instigated the young ex-samurai Nishino to carry out his daring act of assassination of a leading public figure.

Miyake Setsurei, prominent critic of the day, described Mori after his death as an enlightened individualist during his earlier years and a reactionary conservative in his later years. This seemingly incompatibility of the "two Moris" was perhaps a natural consequence of the period when Japan was evolving from a feudal state into a modern nation on the western model. Mori's unique personality complicated his image even more. He

In Japan, just after the Meiji Restoration.

Some of the students sent to England by the Satsuma clan. Mori is seated
the center.

Mori, second from left, as Ambassador to Washington in the early 1870s.

Mori as Minister of Education.

always acted resolutely, expressing his oftentimes radical opinions frankly, contrary to the subtleties of traditional Japanese decorum. He was portrayed by a historian as the consummate man of action, an evergreen standing nobly on a snow-covered mountain.

This dichotomy in the image of Mori became intertwined with the complexities of the modernization of Japanese education and society in the latter half of the nineteenth century. Why, for example, were his conservative tendencies and beliefs virtually ignored upon his death, when the publicity concentrated on his act of defiance of Imperial tradition and his progressive plan to reform the school system? Why, also, was he considered by some critics a liberal individualist and a guardian of religious freedom during his earlier years who evolved into a nationalist in the latter period? Why did his life end in tragedy? In order to answer these legitimate questions, we must return to the beginning of the life of one of Japan's greatest educators.

Twenty-one years before the Meiji Restoration terminated the Tokugawa era of military rule, Mori Arinori was born into a samurai, or warrior, family of the Satsuma clan in Kyushu. At the time of his birth in 1847, few leaders of his clan could foresee that the well-entrenched Tokugawa regime, already in power for over two hundred years, would shortly thereafter come to an abrupt end. Nor could they envision the unique role the Satsuma clan was to play in the final dramatic scenes of the Tokugawa era and the opening acts of the Meiji Restoration in 1868.

Along with other boys of his privileged status, Mori entered the clan school, Zoshikan, at the age of eleven. What would eventually prove to be of unusual significance in this young warrior's life was his first encounter, during his lessons, with radical political concepts through a book written by the controversial figure Hayashi Shihei. This author of a critical essay called "National Sovereignty and Maritime Powers" was arrested for his outspoken opposition to the Tokugawa shogunate's policy of national isolation, under which Japan was held in virtual seclusion from international currents during the extended hegemony of the Tokugawa family.

Hayashi argued that Japan was itself a maritime nation inextricably linked to other Pacific and Atlantic nations. To counter western colonialization, it was therefore essential that Japan's national self-defense policy be based on a global perspective, not on isolationism. Since this contention was diametrically opposed to governmental policy, the book was banned. Nevertheless, through Hayashi's writings, Mori learned about anti-government theories.

At the time of Mori's early education, the Satsuma clan had already come to the fore as an opponent of the central government and the Tokugawa regime. From this position clan leaders were eager to introduce western technology, which, despite the ban on foreign ideas, had become known to some extent to the leaders of this Kyushu province located far from the seat of government in Edo (Tokyo). The Satsuma clan had already unexpectedly experienced a painful introduction to modern western military technology as a result of the Namamugi Incident. In 1862, Charles Richardson, a British merchant grudgingly allowed to reside in Japan, unwittingly rode his horse across the path of an advancing Satsuma procession returning home from an official visit to the capital city. A fanatical young samurai, incensed by the insult, attacked the foreigner, ruthlessly hacking him to death. Determined to avenge the murder, British warships later bombarded the capital of Satsuma, the castle town of Kagoshima. Much of the defenseless city was reduced to ashes as the vaunted British navy demonstrated its overwhelmingly superior military capability. The experience was a painful lesson to the Satsuma leadership, exposing how far behind Japan had fallen in comparison to western technology as a result of its seclusion policy.

Chastened by the humiliating event, Satsuma leaders promptly set out to reduce the imbalances between Japanese and western technology. In a harbinger of Japanese reaction to western technical superiority, they established a clan school in 1864 called Yogakko Kaiseisho. The curriculum was designed to teach western languages and culture, in defiance of the national ban on foreign influences enacted by a feudal government no longer able to carry out its mandate to preserve Japanese culture and traditions from external elements. It was this early clan school that Mori Arinori entered to study English.

Meanwhile the impatient Satsuma government decided to proceed one step further in learning from its attackers. It drew up a secret plan to send promising young boys from samurai families to England for the express purpose of studying culture and technology. This represented another daring act of defiance of central government authority. It also demonstrated the progressive nature of certain local clan leaders who recognized the inevitability of the demise of feudal military government. In this particular distant southern clan, arrangements were made for fourteen young boys, including Mori, to clandestinely board an English ship off a Satsuma port in May 1865 for a long and arduous journey halfway around the globe to England.

At the age of eighteen, Mori Arinori arrived in London, assigned to study marine surveying. He was promptly immersed in the study of history, physics, chemistry, and mathematics under the tutelage of Professor Alexander Williamson at the University of London. Although Mori applied himself diligently to his studies, exhibiting a natural talent for mathematics, he soon became restless concentrating only on western technology. His interest slowly gravitated from the natural sciences to political thought and principles. He became particularly interested in the relationship between the private and public sectors in England, best illustrated by the Industrial Revolution and the ensuing growth of private industry. He confessed in a letter to his brother in 1867 that he had decided to redirect his course of study from technology to the modern concepts of the "foundation of the state"—that is, government. A visit to Russia during the summer months strengthened his convictions.

Gradually Mori's interest in analyses critical of parliamentary institutions in England and the United States heightened, along with criticisms of the Czarist Russian government. According to one biographer, Kimura Rikio, the individual who played the most prominent role in nurturing these budding interests of the youthful Japanese was Laurance Oliphant, Mori's official guarantor in England. As a rising British diplomat, he had previously been assigned briefly to Japan, where he was attacked and wounded by a *rōnin*, a masterless samurai, in a well-known protest against foreign intrusion into Japan.

In July 1867, Oliphant abruptly resigned from the British government in order to join the Order of the Brotherhood of New Life, led in the United States by Thomas Lake Harris. Harris was a leader of this Swedenborgian movement, an obscure

Christian sect that bitterly denounced contemporary American society. Sect leaders railed against the materialistic proclivities of American Christianity that had betrayed the unselfish love of God as expressed in the Bible in their greed to satisfy personal desires. Selfless service to others and unselfish love of man exemplified by Christ's love was the only source of regeneration of American society, according to the teachings of the sect.

Under the strong influence of Swedenborgianism, Oliphant quit his official government position as an act of protest against the British Parliament. He was convinced that his government had fallen under the control of a few politicians and their followers who manipulated legal institutions to promote and protect their personal interests. He set out for the United States determined to establish a political utopia far from England. As another historian, Hayashi Takeji, astutely pointed out, Mori was unquestionably influenced by his guarantor's criticism of prevailing western society and government, about which he had been originally dispatched by his clan to learn in order to lead feudal Japan into the modern world. It is a great historical irony that Mori would be exposed to currents critical of advanced western Christian societies that inevitably led him to assume a skeptical attitude toward western utilitarianism and government.

Under the guidance of Oliphant, Mori and several other Japanese students from the Satsuma clan studying in England traveled to the small, isolated Swedenborgian community in the state of New York during the summer of 1867. For them, the rigid discipline of the sect, which denied private property and demanded absolute loyalty to Harris in daily communal work and prayer, was an essential preparatory stage in the rejuvenation of feudal Japan. The spectacle of the young Japanese from privileged samurai class washing clothes, cooking food, and carrying out other menial daily chores was a far cry from the original intent of Satsuma clan leaders when they chose these young boys to learn from the West. The image of a noble samurai washing dishes would be incomprehensible in Japanese society.

The peculiar life Mori experienced during his initial period in the West surely must have stirred within him mixed emotions. For example, on his trip to Russia he felt universal love to be embodied in a kindly innkeeper who invited him to attend a

Christian church service, an event he never forgot, although he had strong feelings of anxiety and incompatibility toward Christianity. Nevertheless, his participation in the activities of the Swedenborgian Christian community represented a drastic change in his life. The devotees' practice, in the name of Christ, of unselfish love and labor in their tightly knit village was perhaps reminiscent of Mori's upbringing in the samurai spirit of Confucian stoicism and self-restraint, the famous *bushidō*, or "way of the warrior." Oliphant introduced Mori to the group as a "living Confucius." The new lifestyle, although Christian, may have fit this image.

In December of 1867, Mori and his colleagues, who were in the West to prepare for this historic moment in Japanese history, learned of the collapse of the feudal Tokugawa regime. It was quickly replaced by the restoration of Emperor Meiji in what was to mark the initial stages of the modernization of Japan. Upon the advice of the sect leader, Harris, Mori returned to Japan in June of 1868 at the still youthful age of twenty-one to join the new government. In his mind it was an opportunity to realize his great dream of establishing a society of equality based on the principles of unselfish love.

Upon his return to Japan, Mori met with Iwakura Tomomi, one of the prominent figures in the new government. Iwakura, recognizing the potential in Mori, persuaded him to abandon his western clothes, presenting him with a traditional Japanese kimono. The older statesman was concerned that the westernized appearance of the young returnee would invite an attack by radical nationalists intent on expelling foreign influence. It was a rude awakening to Mori after three years in the West. His native country in many ways seemed alien to him.

The Satsuma clan quickly assumed a leading role in the Meiji government. Since Mori, a Satsuma samurai, had just returned from the West with a rare fluency in English, he was immediately appointed to a high position in the foreign department. However, the intense internal struggles for power and direction greatly restricted his opportunities to exert influence. He soon became frustrated.

Coinciding with his appointment to the foreign department, Mori was also assigned to a research unit studying parliamentary institutions. This topic was of particular interest to him as an outgrowth of his fascination with Western governments. Apparently Mori took an active role in the deliberations since he was subsequently appointed chairman of a legislative council organized to develop new governmental agencies. He was still only twenty-two years old; such was the peculiar nature of the fledgling government.

Mori impetuously launched a campaign to rectify political and social conditions in Japan. Accordingly he proposed to the committee the highly controversial abolition of sword-bearing. The samurai class traditionally wore swords, denoting their privileged position in the Tokugawa military government. To Mori, this symbolic act epitomized the inequality and injustices of Japanese feudal society. He himself had already given up the practice, much to the consternation of some other samurai.

The radical proposal was immediately rejected by all members of the council as an outrageous attempt to emasculate the status of the powerful samurai families. Mori's life was threatened over the incident, and he was forced to retire from his post in the new government in Tokyo and return to his home in Kagoshima. To a young man still in his early twenties, the long journey from Kyushu to England, Russia, the United States, Tokyo, and back to Kyushu over a dramatic four-year period must have been something to contemplate as he settled down to the quiet life of a teacher of English to sons of samurai families of his Satsuma clan.

Within a very short time, however, Mori was recalled to Tokyo by a government unable to find qualified Japanese for diplomatic posts. Suddenly Mori found himself being appointed the first diplomat representing the Japanese government in Washington as Japan and the United States officially recognized each other. In effect, at the age of twenty-three, Mori Arinori became the first Japanese ambassador to the United States.

Characteristically, the youthful new diplomat in Washington set out to deepen his understanding of western culture by cultivating a wide variety of leading intellectual figures in American education and government. He also began to collect materials and to develop relationships with individuals he thought could help advise Japan on the reformation of education. In the campaign to modernize Japanese society, the government had given Mori that specific assignment among his official duties.

During his short diplomatic career in Washington, Mori invited a number of American intellectuals to express their opinions and to extend advice on the reformation of Japanese education. Thirteen responded to his questionnaire. Perhaps in response to those questions and the general lack of knowledge among Americans about Japan and its institutions, Mori wrote a book in English entitled *Education in Japan*. From this study, which is one of the first books ever written in English by a native Japanese, we can gain insights into Mori's view of civilization and Japanese history.

Mori divided Japanese history into four stages, analyzing the legal and moral bases of each: the age of mythology, the age of the Mikado, the samurai period, and the Meiji era. Throughout Japanese history, Mori recognized the unbroken lineage of the Imperial system and the leading role of the Imperial family. Nevertheless he also pointed out that the Imperial system violated moral law by such accepted social practices as the keeping of concubines, and that the major weakness of the Japanese political and social systems was caused by unjust marital practices and the vague legal basis of succession to the throne.

The role of the Satsuma and Choshu clans in the overthrow of the Tokugawa Shogunate also came under scrutiny by Mori. He claimed that their maneuvering against the central government, culminating in armed rebellion, represented an immoral *coup d'état*. Therefore the new government, under the powerful influence of Choshu and Satsuma leaders, should assume responsibility for establishing an environment of political morality. The new Meiji government, he maintained, must move progressively forward on a firm moral and legal foundation.

In the process of developing a just and modern state and eradicating feudalism, Mori claimed that the emerging patterns unfortunately were responses more to external pressure from other countries than to internal awareness by Japanese themselves of their needs. That led him to conclude that the youth of the country who had been exposed to western culture were in a unique position, as young Japanese intellectuals, to take the initiative internally to bring about the necessary reforms. This was obviously Mori's justification for his own activities.

In another book, *Religious Freedom in Japan,* written in English in the U.S., Mori claimed that freedom of religion must be recognized as a natural right of man. It was therefore the responsibility of the government, he said, to protect that right. To counter critics who argued that Christianity provoked social unrest in Japan, Mori argued that progress historically develops through a continual succession of experiments and reforms. Disorders are merely temporary pages in the lengthy book of social progress. The concept of freedom of religion was deeply ingrained in Mori. Later, as Minister of Education, he visited schools, where he called upon local teachers and officials not to suppress the free development of religious thought. He urged school administrators to encourage a school environment that nourished freedom of the mind.

In 1872, Mori was suddenly recalled home after a delegation of government officials from Tokyo submitted critical reports concerning his opposition to official governmental instructions. Upon his return, he directed his boundless energies toward a host of activities. Among them, the founding of the Meirokusha (Meiji Six Society), an organization of leading intellectuals, remains one of his most progressive contributions. Named after the sixth (*roku*) year of the Meiji era, it included such distinguished figures as Fukuzawa Yukichi, Nakamura Masanao, and Nishi Amane. With the aim of enlightening the public on legitimate currents of reform, Mori and others used the organization's journal *Meiroku Zasshi* to challenge the existing social order, which they saw as overrun by feudal customs governing the conduct of the people. Typical of the topics covered was "The Duty of Intellectuals" and "A Critique of the Plan for the Establishment of an Elected Parliament."

In one of his memorable legacies, Mori attacked the inequality of the sexes in Japanese society, especially the accepted practice of marriage in which the husband maintained a concubine along with a legal wife. As a bold act of defiance against tradition and as an example to others, Mori entered into matrimony in what is considered the first western-style wedding ceremony in Japan, denoting mutual obligations between equals. With the governor of Tokyo, Okubo Tadahiro, and other distinguished guests as witnesses, Mori demonstrated through action his view of civilization and a deeply rooted disdain for conventional morals.

In yet another radical proposal, Mori advocated replacing Japanese with English as the national language, a suggestion that sparked considerable controversy. He had developed the idea of essentially a dual-track school system in which a disciplined moral education was mandatory at the earlier levels. The higher levels would be devoted to scientific studies based on the principles of academic freedom. For the progress of Japanese civilization, Mori concluded that the Japanese language should be used in ordinary daily life, and English in the school as a vehicle for scientific studies. This truly revolutionary proposal was often used as an example of Mori's extremism by those nationalists who opposed both Mori and the diffusion of western culture.

Individual rights were also strenuously defended by Mori, and his concern carried over even into the area of national finance. When the Meiji government decided to reduce by one third the annual stipend granted to all former samurai in exchange for a one-time payment and devised a unique way to finance the huge expense, Mori opposed the plan on the grounds that it impinged on the individual rights of the ex-samurai, who had no involvement in the decision affecting their lives.

Officials were dispatched by the government to the United States to float a loan on the money markets to raise funds for the project. Mori, then serving in Washington as Japan's top diplomat, opposed his government's flotation of a foreign bond since the whole plan violated individual rights. Facing Mori's persistent objection, the Japanese financial officers went to England to carry out their plan. This episode revealed how strongly Mori held on to his convictions, even though they were divorced from reality at times. To him, individual rights were indispensable to the progress of society and mankind.

In his private life, Mori pursued a just society by introducing modern concepts of marriage and respecting the rights of women, since he firmly believed that the ideal society was based on the family: a moral society could not be achieved without the recognition of the rights of women in the family.

Mori's rigid attitude toward women's rights was epitomized by an encounter he had later, as ambassador to China, with a leading Chinese official. The official questioned Mori about the positive and negative features of Asian countries in comparison with western societies. Much to the surprise of the Chinese leader, Mori replied that Asians were no better than animals. He explained that although women were the mothers of all human beings and should be respected accordingly, they were treated otherwise in Asian societies. When asked if his opinion was based on Christian convictions, Mori replied that he had no specific religion. His only principles of life were that people should follow the path of righteousness without infringing upon the rights of others, including women.

In contrast to his progressive stance on certain issues, Mori opposed the direct election of the Diet as a representative form of government, which he felt would deteriorate into a meaningless body dominated by special-interest groups. Under the earlier influence of the Englishman Oliphant, Mori had developed a skeptical attitude toward the abuses of western parliamentary institutions and of the utilitarian features of advanced societies. He believed that democratic institutions evolved from a moral base in the citizenry. Therefore, rather than impose a western-type parliament on a people incapable of supporting it, the first and foremost problem facing the new Meiji government was to build a solid foundation of social morality. In this attitude he differed from several other leading figures of the day. It was in fact several years later, when Mori served in the prestigious post of Ambassador to the Court of St. James's in London, that he reversed his attitude, recognizing the importance of a representative form of government.

Mori also took issue with the great Fukuzawa over another topic, the latter's widely acclaimed "Theory of Intellectuals" (*Gakusha Shokubunron*). In this treatise Fukuzawa advocated a special role for the intellectual classes serving as a buffer between the state and society by guiding public opinion in the proper direction. The result would be a prosperous nation. However, Mori contended that intellectuals like himself should serve within administrative organs of state in order to promote the public welfare. He could not envision how a special social strata of intellectuals acting outside the state apparatus could bring about progress for all. People blessed with intellectual ability should be responsive to the needs of the state by becoming an integral part of its administration, in Mori's view of government.

Another of the wide-ranging activities that interested Mori during his shortened career was the Commercial Institute (Shoho Koshujo), which he established with his own funds in 1875. During his second sojourn in the United States, Mori recognized the vital importance of education in the success of a nation's economy. At that time the Japanese government placed great stress on education in law, engineering, and medical science. Because of the strong influence during the Tokugawa period of Confucianism, which viewed economic activity with disdain, education related to economics and commerce had received little attention. Thus, Japan was inadequately prepared to expand its commercial activities under the Meiji government.

Mori's new institute was specifically designed to fill that gap. Upon his appointment as Ambassador to China, the institute's management was turned over to the Tokyo Chamber of Commerce, and shortly thereafter it became the center of commercial education in Japan. It was eventually to become Hitotsubashi University, a leading institution in contemporary Japan in the areas of finance, trade, and commerce. Mori's foresight more than one hundred years ago was thus to play a catalytic role in Japan's spectacular transformation into a supereconomic power in the twentieth century.

Among Mori's many contributions to Japan, his views on education are understandably of the greatest importance since he is considered the father of the modern Japanese school system. One of the first opportunities we have of analyzing his personal views on education came in his 1879 lecture on education for physical development before the Japan Academy. It was the initial revelation of his attitudes toward a national philosophy of education. In this speech he claimed that the role of education was to develop the intellectual, moral, and physical development of the individual. This broad approach to education indicated the influence Herbert Spencer, author of the classic *Education: Intellectual, Moral and Physical*, exerted on Mori. The two had met in London when Mori visited Spencer during his diplomatic service.

Mori made the curious claim that because the Japanese people were lacking in physical stature, it was extremely difficult to cultivate their intellectual and moral development. Since he felt that the progress of educational development was dependent on a strong physical foundation, he called for the introduction of a military-based physical exercise program in the nation's new school system; this regimen was, ultimately, implemented by Mori as Minister of Education. His strong views on physical education of a military nature attracted criticism.

Underlying Mori's philosophy of education was his antagonism toward Confucianism, which had exerted a dominant influence over education throughout the 250-year Tokugawa Shogunate. The basic method of Confucianist learning was simply to memorize and reproduce intricate passages from classical texts indoctrinating a specific discipline of thought. Mori was adamantly opposed to instilling any specific religious, political, or philosophical doctrine in students; rather, education must provide the opportunity for students to develop their own way of thinking. Since his attitude negated that of conservative believers in Confucianism—and there were many—Mori became a target of criticism.

In September 1879, just prior to Mori's ambassadorial assignment to England, the highly progressive Education Ordinance (*Kyoiku Rei*) was enacted under the leadership of Tanaka Fujimaro, a high official of the Ministry of Education. Mori's liberal influence was evidenced even in this early educational law. As a member of the Iwakura Mission, Tanaka had previously made a school inspection trip to the United States and Europe. During his visit to the U.S., Mori, the top Japanese diplomat in Washington, had accompanied the delegation of dignitaries on several school visits. The senior member and leader of the group, Kido Takayoshi, however, regarded Mori as a Westernized young radical promoting American-style education for Japan. In fact, Kido reported back to the government that if Mori were ever appointed to a post in the Ministry of Education, it would do more harm than good.

The Education Ordinance drafted by Tanaka contained several basic ideas of Mori's. For example, the placing of elementary schools under the control of prefectural governments rather than the central Ministry of Education, with a local district supervisor maintaining the actual administrative responsibility, was a rare instance of educational decentralization in Japan. It was no coincidence that Mori was well aware of the highly decentralized system of education in the United States.

Tanaka's national educational plan was principally aimed at the broad diffusion of elementary education. Mori differed somewhat: his educational plan, which would be adopted later, was designed to produce manpower required by the state. The schools would be organized into three levels corresponding to the existing social strata of the lower, middle, and upper classes. Mori regarded a national financing plan as an essential ingredient to ensure that the school fulfilled the requirements of the state—a perspective he gained while serving as ambassador to Great Britain.

When Mori arrived in England in 1880 to assume the coveted diplomatic assignment at the center of the most powerful empire in the world, political events were transpiring at a rapid pace in Japan. During his four-year tour, there was an enormous amount of jockeying for power at the seat of government in Tokyo. Former clan leaders struggled for supremacy in determining the direction of the Meiji government. Shortly after Mori left the country in 1881, the leadership changed hands when the progressive Okuma Shigenobu was forced to resign his Cabinet post, although the new leaders agreed to the formation of an elected national parliament in 1890. The succeeding government was led by a coalition of former leaders of Mori's Satsuma clan and the Choshu clan.

A new constitution was required to lay the foundation for the beginnings of parliamentary government from 1890. Ito Hirobumi from the Choshu clan became the central figure in drawing up the provisions. Just at that time, Mori, always interested in Western parliaments, addressed the issue of the relationship between representative government and education, along with the revision of the unequal treaties signed previously by the Japanese and foreign governments when Japan was in a weakened state. According to biographer Sonoda Hidehiro,

Mori promoted a form of nationalistic education in his view of the central role of the state. He saw education as an instrument to serve the state.

The state, then, became the focus of the aims and purposes of Japanese education, according to Mori, who based that conclusion on his analysis of the development of civil societies. No group of people, he argued, has ever been uniformly endowed with intelligence, morality, 'and physical development. In order to protect the weak from the strong, laws are made by societies, which evolved as human intelligence improved. Thus the cultivation of intelligence is a matter of critical importance to all societies and one of the major justifications for compulsory education financed by the public.

Since there are inequalities among people, some form of government must be designed to serve all of the citizenry. Using his experiences in the West, Mori concluded that Western legislative bodies, although elected directly by the public, did not reflect the will of the entire electorate but only the interests of the minority from the better classes. This belief derived from his early period in the West under the influence of Oliphant and Harris of the Swedenborgian sect, who held antagonistic attitudes toward parliamentary forms of government.

Mori's critical stance toward representational government is related to his view of the Imperial system. The Emperor stood at the very apex of the state. Indeed, at a press conference upon his departure as Ambassador to England, he expressed his deep conviction that the progress of Japan depended on two historical pillars: broad support for the Imperial tradition and independence from foreign colonial control. These two factors would enable Japan to progress by absorbing foreign elements in the modernization process while maintaining its cultural identity. Comparing Japan's history and culture with those of western nations, he concluded that a parliament consisting of enlightened representatives indirectly chosen would best serve the interests of the nation and the Emperor.

Japanese culture also contained characteristics superior to those of western societies, specifically fraternal love or paternalism. The individualism of western societies debased the culture into a form of utilitarianism, whereas the ties that bound Japanese

society together were based on mutual affection and consideration for others. In his utopian view of a modern Japanese society,
Mori justified a form of government contrasting with that prevalent in the West, in which an elected parliament with powerful
leaders in fact represented a minority class of landowners. The
challenge that lay ahead of Japan was to construct a modern
educational system that avoided the defects of western political
institutions while adapting to and benefiting from the virtues
of Japanese traditions.

In the year 1882, Ito Hirobumi, the most prominent figure
in Japanese politics, then studying German constitutional law
in Vienna, met Mori, who was visiting the Continent as ambassador to England, in a Paris hotel. In one of the most significant
discussions in modern Japanese history, the two exchanged opinions about the future of Japanese education. At this meeting of
these two great Japanese figures, Mori agreed to accept Ito's offer
of appointment as the first Minister of Education in Ito's new
cabinet.

Mori outlined his view of the state and education, which impressed Ito. At that time Ito supported a new constitution based
on Imperial authority. Education was intended to produce citizens who supported the constitution and maintained peace and
social order. Education, rather than government organs such
as the police or the army, would be the major instrument to
keep public order. Ito also opposed Confucian principles of education, advocated by Motoda Nagazane, entailing the mere
memorization of passages from the classics as the goal of education. He also supported Mori's idea of introducing a military
form of physical training in the schools.

Prior to Mori's appointment as Minister of Education, the
top educational figure in the Japanese government held a position that was not considered very influential. It was at times
not even filled. Mori insisted that the new position be one of
high esteem and responsibility. With Ito's concurrence, Mori
resigned his ambassadorship to the prestigious Court of St.
James's to return home to undertake the construction of a new
national school system.

Initially Motoda and other conservatives opposed Mori's
appointment as Minister of Education. One of the factors be-

hind the opposition was the suspicion that followed Mori to his death: that he was a Christian. Perhaps upon the recommendation of Motoda, the Emperor Meiji himself recommended a conservative, Tani Tateki, as Minister of Education. Rejecting the opposition, Ito assumed individual responsibility for the decision to appoint Mori to guide Japan into the modern era; such were the strong ties formed at their fateful meeting in Paris the year before.

After his return to Japan from England in March 1884, and prior to his appointment as Minister of Education in late 1885, Mori was thrust into the deliberations on the bill for the new constitution then under consideration by the Privy Council. Curiously, he immediately assumed the conservative position against Ito's proposal that the Emperor had the authority to enforce the laws of the land with the approval of the new legislative body, the Imperial Diet. He opposed a constitution that would not recognize the Emperor's ultimate authority over that of the Diet.

Mori also opposed Ito's proposals, then under study, that clearly defined the individual's rights and obligations, essential in any constitutional framework. On the contrary, Mori argued that the individual in Japanese society had responsibilities to the Emperor, to be differentiated from any rights. Thus it was unnecessary to include a "rights" provision in the new constitution, a position supported by the arch-conservative advisor to the Emperor, Motoda Nagazane, who also supported Mori's opposition to voting requirements of majority rule that would encourage the evils of partisan politics. Mori's movement back and forth on certain issues from the progressive to the conservative has defied a rational analysis by his biographers.

Mori's attempt to modernize Japan based on traditional Japanese customs with the Imperial system at the center was strongly influenced by his view of the inherent differences among people. He was convinced that those gifted with superior qualities (presumably such as himself) should serve the national government as "enlightened leaders." Those with less talent should serve as local leaders of government, while at the bottom levels of government the least able could carry out routine work. An education system would have to be constructed to meet the demands of the state arranged in this hierarchical structure.

As the new Minister of Education, Mori plunged into the position with a rapid succession of new regulations designed to transform Japanese education from top to bottom. From March through April of 1886, new regulations for Imperial universities (*Teikoku Daigaku Rei*), teacher training colleges (*Shihan Gakkō Rei*), secondary education (*Chūgakkō Rei*), and elementary education (*Shōgakkō Rei*) were all issued from the Ministry of Education. For the first time in Japanese history, the aims and purposes of schooling were officially defined.

The central doctrine established by the new Minister of Education was that education must be conducted in a national school system under state control and financed primarily by the state. Education should be aimed at the welfare of both the individual and the nation. Lower-level education was intended to promote individual awareness of one's rights and duties as a loyal citizen, whereas upper-level education was intended to promote the welfare of the nation through the education of a class for national leadership. Lower-level education would be strictly controlled by the state. In contrast, freedom of research and study would govern education at the higher levels. A normal-school system to train teachers for the lower schools under the strict control of the government would be organized separately from the relatively free university system.

One of the most significant elements of Mori's attitude toward education was his distinction between learning (*gakumon*) and education (*kyoiku*). In various lectures he took the opportunity to spell out how they differed. Education meant to him the intellectual, moral, and physical training received under the guidance of one's teacher. On the other hand, learning involved the process of individual development. For example, education at the Imperial universities represented the process of learning, with the individual essentially responsible for his own development. At the lower school levels the student was educated under the specific instruction of teachers.

The ordinance governing the establishment of national universities clearly defined their purpose as offering curricula correspondent to the needs of the nation. Upper secondary education was designed to prepare students for the university or for business. The aims of elementary education were not so clearly defined. Nevertheless, in a speech at a normal school in Wakayama in 1887, the Minister called for an elementary education that would develop the child's personality and a code of conduct for loyal subjects of the Emperor.

The success of the new national elementary schools depended to a large extent on the quality of the teachers, which in turn greatly determined the success of the nation in international competition, both military and economic, according to Mori. Because of the fundamental role of the teacher in the well-being of the nation, Mori devoted himself to the reforming of the normal school system. He revealed his intentions in a speech at Saitama Normal School in December 1885, prior to his appointment as Minister of Education.

A teacher should not be judged from the perspective of the subject matter being taught. Rather, a teacher's worth must be valued according to his disposition reflected in three traits: obedience, friendship, and dignity. Obedience (*junryo*) involved faithfully following the regulations of the school and the instructions of the principal; dignity (*iju*) concerned the ability to train students to follow the instructions of the teacher; and friendship (*shin'ai*) was the process of cultivating good manners among human beings. To develop these essential ingredients of the good teacher, an intensive training program on a military pattern should be employed based on the army's demand for obedience to orders, the dignity of an officer controlling his men, and the camaraderie among soldiers. Accordingly, Mori introduced into the new normal-school system a military type of physical training and mandatory dormitory life.

Mori also considered important the element of student selection for normal-school entry. In order to secure carefully selected applicants, he called for their recommendation by the local mayor from among the best students in the community, who would then be employed as local teachers upon graduation. In order to fulfill the needs of the country, each prefecture would provide the financing. He concluded his speech by describing the ideal teacher as an "educational priest in the image of Buddhism."

As a rationalist, Mori was deeply interested in the effective administrative and financial management of the school system. To accomplish this, he placed the control and financing of the Imperial universities and preparatory secondary schools under the authority of the national government. Elementary schools would come under the control and financing of local bodies, with local governments providing assistance to the needy.

Although Mori's goal was a compulsory school system for all, attendance remained persistently below fifty percent. He criticized such a condition, warning that with that rate of illiteracy Japan could not maintain its independence in diplomatic affairs, nor could it build a strong foundation for the nation. He urged each local community to establish an elementary-school system with mathematics as the primary subject to give all children the ability to make decisions on a rational basis.

He defined his approach to education as *keizai shugi*, or the economic principle, in which the result justified the effort. This principle was to be applied in every aspect of the school, from teaching methods to school administration. Thus his economic principle extended far beyond school finance into such areas as responsibility, in which every officer of the school system who had the authority to appoint had to accept responsibility for that appointee in a manner consistent with the relationships that exist in a family.

He placed responsibility for local education with an Education Committee consisting of local educators and influential members of the community. Their role was somewhat akin to that of an American school board, which collected funds to finance the school, recommended the principal, and provided general advice for the overall operation of the school. Mori even made such detailed, and somewhat bizarre, recommendations as the planting of certain types of trees along the roads that could later be sold at high prices to make valuable furniture. It was all part of his scheme to conduct a national school system within the very limited means of the state's budget.

Mori's attitude toward the sensitive issues of loyalty and patriotism deserves special consideration. As mentioned previously, he was highly critical of Confucian educational practices and moral discipline. Nor did he relinquish his basic support for religious freedom. In many speeches he recognized the right of teachers to hold personal religious and political beliefs, but warned that it was improper for them to impart those beliefs to their students. This caveat was specifically aimed at eliminating Confucian doctrine from its traditionally influential role in the schools.

Moral education as Mori perceived it concerned the relationships between human beings. Confucian precepts regulated the hierarchical relationship between lord and vassal, father and son, husband and wife, elder and younger. Mori believed that the basis of modern society was close human relationships of a horizontal nature between people with no concern for Buddha or any philosopher. He introduced ethics into the course on morals in an attempt to replace the course (called *shushin*), used to impart specific moral indoctrination, notably that related to Confucianism and Shintoism.

The writer of the new morals textbook under Mori, Nose Sakae, described the Minister's view on morals education as personally revealed to him. Morality should not be based on any religion, philosophy, or doctrine of a specific individual. Rather, society is based on the interpersonal relationships among its members. When a mutually beneficial relationship is established between individuals, the society is at peace. Otherwise it is in conflict.

Friendship was one of the characteristics of Japanese society that Mori considered to be a positive element in comparison with western societies. Therefore he considered friendliness an essential ingredient of the teacher's disposition. It was the duty of the teacher to nurture mutual assistance based on friendship through the new ethics course.

The arch-Confucianist Motoda criticized Mori's ethics course, claiming that it was too abstract to develop a loyal Japanese subject. Other figures of the day also expressed dissatisfaction with the course, since it did not include loyalty to the Emperor. These outspoken critics reflected widespread opposition to the Minister of Education by most conservatives on the issues of loyalty and patriotism, which inextricably involved morality.

Mori struggled with the related problem of how to develop fidelity to the Imperial state rather than to the Emperor himself. In a bill drafted by him defining the purposes of educational reform, he called for loyalty to the state in order for Japan to compete successfully in the international arena of diplomacy. He felt that people in the West united in the defense of their country when threatened, regardless of social or religious background. However, because the Meiji government was autocratically ruled by a few powerful figures, individual Japanese could not conceive of what the state actually represented. This was to him one of the major unresolved problems of education: how to develop a sense of nationalism through the schools without resorting to indoctrination.

In order to nurture patriotism and love of country, Mori turned not to the Emperor but to the historical symbol of the long reign of the Japanese Imperial system. For him there was no alternative to building that critical sense of nationhood other than the Imperial Family itself. The Imperial tradition consequently became a symbol of nationhood in Mori's new school system.

The distinction between the Emperor, regarded by Confucianists and Shintoists as a *revered deity*, and the Imperial tradition as a symbol of Japanese nationhood was of great importance to the architect of the national school system of Japan. It also defined for him the mission of the schools in producing loyal subjects, not to be confused with absolute obedience to the Emperor. Regrettably, it was also a major factor in bringing this great educator's life to a tragic end. The assassin's dagger was aimed at destroying Japan's first Minister of Education, who rejected predetermined indoctrination of any nature in his quest to build a modern united nation based on Japanese cultural traditions.

As one of the greatest educators Japan has ever produced, Mori Arinori was clearly ahead of his time. The very year following his death, the Japanese government issued the Imperial Rescript on Education, which eventually became the symbol of ultranationalism and Emperor-worship indoctrination in the schools. It reflected the essence of Confucianism and Shintoism, the very concepts Mori sought to expel from the schools.

On the other hand, his structure for education remained essentially in place until the postwar era. The lower-level schools provided a solid basic education for all with a competent teaching corps graduating from the teacher training institutions. Higher education produced loyal graduates prepared to serve the nation in its administrative organs. Among them was the new Ministry of Education, designed by Mori to maintain Japan's first national school system. One can only conjecture about the course of Japan's history in the prewar era if the first Minister of Education, Mori Arinori, had lived to direct it beyond the inaugural period.

The Life of Mori Arinori

1847   Born into a samurai family of the Satsuma clan.

1856   Entered Zoshikan, the clan school.

1864   Entered Kaiseijo, the clan school of western studies, to study English.

1866   Sent by the Satsuma clan to study in London.

1867   Traveled to the U.S. to join the Swedenborgian community.

1868   Returned to Japan; appointed Vice Counsellor of Foreign Affairs.

1869   Introduced a bill for the abolition of sword-wearing, and returned to Satsuma upon defeat of the bill.

1870   Ordered back to government service; appointed the first Japanese ambassador to the United States.

1872   Published *Religious Freedom in Japan*.

1873   Published *Education in Japan*.

1875   Established the Shoho Koshujo, the Commercial Institute; appointed chief representative to the government of China.

1879   Appointed ambassador to the Court of Saint James's, England.

1883   Published *Nihon Seifu Daigiseitai Ron* [On a Representative System of Government].

1884   Assigned as an adviser to the Ministry of Education.

1885   Appointed Minister of Education in the first Ito Cabinet.

1886   Imperial University Ordinance, Normal School Ordinance, Elementary School Ordinance, and Middle School Ordinance promulgated.

1888   Participated in the deliberation of the Imperial Constitution in the Privy Council.
1889   Assassinated by Buntaro Nishino.

About the Author

Terumichi Morikawa was born in 1945 in Hyogo Prefecture, and completed the doctoral course in education at Tokyo Kyoiku University in 1974. He is currently Associate Professor at Saitama University. His publications (in Japanese) include *The New Educational History of Japan* (1984) and *The Modern Imperial Regime and Japanese Education*.

Naruse Jinzo in 1917.

Naruse Jinzo
[1858–1919]
Kuni Nakajima

Naruse Jinzo is recognized as a great educator of women in modern Japan. He founded the distinguished Japan Women's University in 1901 at the age of forty-two in order to put his ideals of education into practice. Its foundation marked a turning point in promoting the quality of education for women, a feat achieved only through a long and arduous struggle. Naruse had to face public criticism and indifference—attitudes which reflected the prevalent opinion concerning female education in those days—as he led the movement for establishing a higher educational institution for women.

The history of women's education in modern Japan can be divided into three periods: from 1872 to the 1890s, when the Gakusei (Education Law), the first modern national school system, was established; from 1900 to 1945; and from the postwar period to the present. It was during the second period that Naruse founded the Japan Women's University as the first higher educational institution for women in the nation.

First of all, it is necessary to consider the condition of women's education during the first phase of its development. This stage occurred when the Meiji government proclaimed the Gakusei, one of its most important policies, which laid the foundation for the modern public educational system and in which provisions for elementary education for all were included. Women, previously less educated than men, were now encouraged to attend school because of the new ideal that everyone should be educated. However, education for women, even at the elementary-school level, showed little advancement. The percentages of school attendance at the beginning of the Gakusei (1872) stood at 39.9 for boys and 15.4 for girls. Even in 1892, twenty years after the proclamation of the Gakusei, the percentage of girls attending school was only 36.4 percent, a low figure compared with 71.6 percent attendance for boys.

During this time, although the public-school structure was gradually being constructed through school legislation such as the Law for Elementary Schools, the Law for Secondary Schools, the Law for Normal Schools, and the Law for Universities, legislation for women's education showed very little progress. No positive policies were under consideration concerning women's education at that time. In fact, when the policy to promote school enrollment during the Gakusei is reviewed, it is evident that at the beginning of modern public education in Japan, girls' education was designed primarily to encourage them to become good wives and mothers, whereas boys were encouraged to learn how to succeed in life.

Separate education for boys and girls was embodied in the new Education Ordinance of 1879: "Boys and girls should not sit together in the same classroom" (Clause 14). Consequently, except for the lower grades of elementary school, boys and girls were educated separately. By the 1880s, a decade after the Gakusei was inaugurated, there were neither coeducational middle nor coed higher schools. The policy of educating boys and girls separately, coupled with the Confucian respect for males, further reinforced this practice. Although the educational system for boys was gradually expanded, that for girls was restricted. For example, in a series of ordinances ratified by school laws on public education, education for girls was not even specifically mentioned.

This negative attitude on the part of the government toward women's education contrasted with the people's desire for an education inspired by western influences, called *bunmei kaika* (civilization and enlightenment) in the Meiji era. Under these circumstances, vocational education was provided for girls at various private institutions, where even science, which was not included in upper-level schools, was taught. Some of the private schools provided education for both sexes. Even girls' schools such as *jogakko* and *onna-juku* (boarding schools for girls) also permitted boys to attend classes.

Naruse in 1884, after his ordination at age 26.

The farewell lecture, 1918.

Because of the eventual enforcement of segregated education even in private institutions, girls could no longer sit together with boys. Nevertheless these private schools for girls came to play an important role in girls' education, especially the Christian schools supported and managed by both foreign missionaries and Japanese. Educational activities offered by schools run by missionaries became an important means of introducing Christianity. Their methods of teaching were almost the same as those in their own countries, with high standards and a unique atmosphere that matched the trend of westernization of the time. Thus, enrollment in these private schools administered by missionaries became the goal for girls from the upper classes. Christian schools for girls administered by Japanese also offered education based upon Christianity but were run on the belief that education for Japanese girls should be conducted by Japanese to provide a proper education. Some of these Christian schools for women even offered higher education, consequently producing graduates who were later actively engaged in various aspects of society.

At the dawn of modern Japan, the development of women's education was thus just in its infancy. The state's educational policy fell short of achieving a modern educational system. It did not conduct regular classroom education on a coeducational basis. However, it did offer private schools an opportunity to provide a flexible education for women.

There were several factors in education for women in which Naruse became interested, and which finally resulted in the establishment of a higher educational institution for women in the midst of the educational climate described above. First of all, his childhood played an important role. Naruse was the eldest son of a lesser samurai family that belonged to the Choshu clan (in what is now Yamaguchi Prefecture), which played an important role during the Meiji Restoration. His father, Naruse Kozaemon, served the family of Mori Kiyoshi, one of the Lord of Choshu's kinsmen. His mother, Utako, also came from a samurai family. The Naruses were well educated in Chinese classics and respected as a family of scholars and educators.

Naruse, having been reared with an appreciation of the great historical changes taking place during the Meiji Restoration, studied at Kenshokan, a feudal school established by the Choshu clan. He then assisted his father at Kajuku, a private school run by his father. However, since his grandmother and mother died by the time he was seven, young Naruse was brought up by a stepmother who came from a merchant family. It seems that Naruse was rather critical of his stepmother since he could not adapt to her different customs. He lost the close family relationship as his sister Hisako, three years his senior, followed by his brother Shin, married and moved away. Then Naruse's father died when the boy was sixteen years old, leaving him to face the grim realities of life, which brought him closer to religious convictions. Under the influence of Confucianism and samurai ethics, and because of his family circumstances, it was quite natural for him to hold the view that women were emotional beings and that men were naturally superior to women. In later years his aunt revealed to him that his natural mother had been a wise and able woman and "an uncommonly clever and talented person." He learned that she had been kind and affectionate as well. Naruse reflected upon this revelation and realized that he had inherited from his mother both her emotional character and her steadfastness.

It is clear that up until his adolescence, Naruse held the image that women were inferior to men. However, his view of women was to undergo a drastic change upon his encounter with Christianity. The Christian concept that all human beings are equal before God prompted Naruse to reconsider his attitudes toward women as inferior beings. As the Christian influence increased, he searched further for a way to resolve this contradiction.

A major impact on Naruse was his eventual conversion to Christianity. After his father's death, he had a chance to meet Sawayama Yasura (1852–1887), from the Kiyoshi samurai family, who had become a Christian preacher after studying in the United States. This meeting took place in 1877, after his father's death, when Naruse was the principal of a local elementary school, a position he assumed after graduation from the Kiyoshi Teachers' Training School. He was very much moved by Christianity and resolved to leave his hometown in order to be baptized into the Christian faith at Sawayama's Osaka Naniwa Church.

Dubbed "the youth carrying a Bible," Naruse was appointed head teacher of Baika (Plum Blossom) Women's School, on the strength of his experiences as a teacher and principal. Baika, presently Baika Women's University, founded by the Osaka Naniwa Church in 1878, was the first mission school in Osaka. "A girls' school for the glory of God; therefore, we must educate women and suit them for the Bible," he wrote in his diary, and took the first steps to devote himself to the improvement of women's education based on Christianity. During this time he married Hattori Misui, who also belonged to the Naniwa Church, and published his first work, *Fujoshi no Shokumu* (*The Duties of Women*). However, his educational policy grounded in Christianity was contrary to the school's policy concerning the administration of the school. Naruse was compelled to resign his job as a teacher and to start a new life as a preacher under Sawayama, who was noted for his advocacy of a self-sufficient church.

In 1886, Naruse became a minister of the Niigata Church. There he resumed his efforts for women's education by founding the Niigata Girls' School with the help of those involved in the churches in the Niigata area. Simultaneously he worked at establishing Hokuetsu Gakkan, a school for boys, and promoted a night school for the parish. Naruse took an active part in church activities and in the development of a young men's association under the church's auspices. He was very much affected by the dedication and self-sacrifice of Mrs. Sawayama, the wives of foreign missionaries, and Japanese women engaged in mission work.

Naruse completely devoted himself to educating women and preaching to those who wanted to believe in Christianity despite prejudice and persecution stemming from the belief among many Japanese that Chrisianity was a perverse religion. He often said that "men's eyes should be opened to the spirit and qualities of women, whose noble values should be appreciated," and that he "wished to develop girls who have the ability for nurturing and giving full play to their natural endowments." It is worth noting that although the Baika Girls' School and the Niigata Girls' School were both mission schools, they were administered by Japanese in spite of all the difficulties in running them.

Naruse was also greatly influenced by the opportunity to study in the United States. In the late 1890s he went to America with the ambition to become more progressive. At the Andover Theological Seminary, he was strongly influenced by the sociologist Dr. M. J. Tucker. During this time a Mr. Leavitt, a friend of Naruse's when he was living in Osaka, helped to pay Naruse's tuition and living costs. While boarding with the Leavitts, Naruse learned much about the ways of living in a Puritan home.

A year later Naruse transferred to Clark University to study pedagogy, specializing in women's education. He often visited American schools and churches in the area and had many opportunities to give lectures. He met with people associated with higher education and became concerned with religion and public-welfare services. He also spent time investigating institutions for the handicapped and published *Modern Paul*, the biography of Sawayama Yasura, whom he had respected as his lifelong teacher. Although he was strongly urged to complete his degree in the United States, Naruse decided to return to Japan at the end of 1894 according to his original plans. He returned with more determination than ever to establish a higher educational institution for women, an idea that had been nurtured by observing American women and their education.

In March of the year after his return, Naruse was appointed principal of Baika Girls' School. The appointment provided him an opportunity to launch a movement for the establishment of a university for women. With the help of Aso Shozo, later to become Naruse's successor as president of Japan Women's University, Naruse completed a thesis on women's education and published it under the title of *Joshi Kyoiku* (*Women's Education*) in February 1896. The work contained Naruse's throughts concerning women's education based on his many years' experience and study in the United States.

He emphasized first of all the idea that women should have a general education in order to develop their full mental and physical potential. Next he stated that higher education in the fields of ethics, general knowledge, art, music, and physical training should be offered in order to develop traits that would make women good mothers and wives. Third, Naruse stressed that education should encourage women to fulfill their obligation to their country. Thus, his views on women's education can be summarized as advocacy of educating girls as human beings, as women, and as citizens of the nation.

Educating women as human beings was Naruse's basic ideal for a higher educational institution, a concept that characterizes his thoughts. This is particularly evident in one of his speeches, "Measures for Promoting Women's Education," in which he emphasized that educating women as human beings should not be confused with educating women as women and as citizens of the nation:

> The main purpose of education is not to teach students how to get on in life, but to develop them as complete human beings. Education is not meant to create a machine that works automatically but to create a person who has the ability to accomplish a certain objective. Education is also not meant to shape students into containers of knowledge, but to equip them with intellectual powers. Simply stated, the aim of education is the full enhancement of one's mental and physical competence to develop a person of nobility and promise. Therefore, an educated person cannot be defined by one's ability to overcome difficulties in life, but by the human character to become adaptable to any situation in life. One should possess all the necessities to accomplish this task no matter what occupation one may have or what situation one may be experiencing. Such are required both in times of war and peace. One's vocation—samurai, peasant, artisan, or merchant—is irrelevant. There should be no distinction between the sexes.

With the above view of human values as a foundation, Naruse promoted women's education as a process of first attempting to develop character with self-consciousness as a human being, then gaining basic knowledge, and finally bringing the individual intellect into full play in order to contribute to the development of Japanese society.

Naruse's educational thoughts can now be summarized. He believed that women have the potential to develop themselves and, therefore, rejected differences of roles between the sexes. He also insisted that "general education should be designed so as to fully develop the various senses in order to form a sound mind in a strong body, and to provide the fundamental abilities required for achieving various duties in life." Reflecting upon this, Naruse thought education should nurture individual characteristics. Therefore he criticized the tendency in women's education of that period to emphasize practical instruction such as housekeeping and sewing.

Naruse observed the role of women in Japanese society and believed that intellectual and physical training should both be promoted as parts of their education. The emphasis on physical training for women in his writings drew much attention. Iwamoto Zenji, the principal of Meiji Jogakko (Meiji Girls' School), is quoted as saying that "the chapter in *Joshi Kyoiku* (*Women's Education*) mentioning physical training for girls impressed me. I wish to see it in practice." Naruse's reference to the physical health of girls as well as the advancement of their intellectual potential was indeed a progressive idea in those days.

Naruse also pointed out in his book the importance of lifelong education. He explained that lifelong education is essential for supporting and improving oneself; therefore it was essential for society to encourage people in their national obligation. He also said that it would make life more comfortable in one's old age.

Joshi Kyoiku was favorably reviewed by *Tokyo Nichinichi Shimbun* (*Tokyo Daily News*), *Rokugo Zasshi* (*A Journal of Enlightenment*), *Jogaku Zasshi* (*Journal for Women's Education*), and other publications for its enlightened view. What significant characteristics did this book possess in comparison with the views of other enlightened thinkers of the early Meiji era concerning women? Fukuzawa Yukichi, one of the leaders of the Meiji enlightenment movement, criticized the feudalistic view of women, but his thoughts were limited regarding the future role of women. Often he simply explained certain situations in generalized terms. On the other hand, Naruse not only criticized society's view of women but also outlined the aims, content, and method for educating women. It can be said that Naruse's many years of direct experience dealing with women's education was reflected in his work.

Another significant characteristic that should be recognized was the strong nationalistic character of his thought. Whenever Naruse referred to intellectual, moral, physical, or vocational training, he was always conscious of Japan as one of the world powers. He emphasized the underdevelopment of women's education in Japan when compared with that in western nations. At the same time, however, he promoted women's education by emphasizing a reevaluation of the Japanese educational system, avoiding the imitation of education in the West.

Naruse insisted that Japan should have its own policy regarding women's education. He justified his position by saying:

> Japan is situated thousands of miles away from western countries, with a vastly different historical background, distinct manners and customs, as well as racial and political differences. Furthermore, it is inappropriate to provide for Japanese women, who are less educated than western women, an education designed specifically for women in the West. Education should be thoroughly compatible with each country's history and conditions. It should also fit the level of its teachers.

Naruse opposed the introduction of the western education typically found in the mission schools that flourished until the early 1890s. He argued that women's education in Japan should not be placed in the hands of foreign missionaries and teachers. At the same tinre, he said, criticism of western education should not be made from a conservative viewpoint.

After the Sino-Japanese War (1894–95), the major western powers, notably Great Britain, France, and Russia, intervened in Far Eastern affairs. This gave an unprecedented impetus to nationalism among the Japanese people. During this period, emphasis on nationalism became a pervasive influence in education. Naruse was no exception. Although his nationalism was as fervent as any, his perspective was not narrowly restricted. For example, he said: "The principles of education are not determined by race or by nation but by humankind and universal ideals. They have nothing to do with differences in governmental systems, whether monarchical or republican, nor are they related to racial factors. Truth is common property, not a private possession." Naruse therefore concluded that the best aspects of western education should be introduced in Japan.

Naruse's book was published amid widespread ignorance

in Japan of the importance of higher education for women. He realized that the economic depression after the Sino-Japanese War made the establishment of higher institutions for women much more difficult. Nevertheless he actively sought out individuals from the financial, governmental, and educational worlds who would support his ideals. He met with those who he hoped would understand his ideals in order to persuade them to adopt his way of thinking. He gained much attention when he wrote: "Half of the human race consists of women. Their potential for supporting and promoting society is more important than is commonly understood. Therefore, the success or failure of women could greatly influence the destiny of the nation."

The opening of schools such as Joshi Eigaku (the Girls' School of English), presently Tsuda Women's College, founded by Tsuda Ume, and the Tokyo Joshi Igakko (presently the Tokyo Women's Medical College, founded by Washiyama Yayoi), as well as Japan Women's University, brought about the dawning of a new age for higher education for women. However, the government eventually changed its policy of dependence upon private schools for girls. It became necessary for the Japanese government, whose status was finally recognized throughout the world, to include girls' schools in the new national policy.

The ordinance of 1899 concerning women's higher education was the first step in the new policy, and it was followed by a series of administrative amendments. The new policy was based upon the concept of developing good wives and mothers. It was enacted during the same period in which a civil law code, the last of the series of laws required of a modern state, was enacted. The civil law affirmed the traditional Japanese patriarchal family system; that is to say, it was the successor to the *ie* system of primogeniture, upon which the basic structure of the Meiji Imperial state was built. The education of good wives and mothers was inseparably related to the *ie* system and to the concept of the "nation as a family," characteristic of the ideology for integrating the society under the Meiji Imperial state.

From this point of view, women were regarded as no more than "females chained to the home." This type of education, aimed at maintaining the *ie* system and ultimately to provide national stability, required women to be obedient, patient, frugal, diligent, chaste, and respectful to their parents. It was derived from Confucianism, under which education for women was regarded as discipline rather than intellectual development, always keeping girls' educational levels lower than those of boys.

The government did not allow girls to enter higher educational institutions except the women's normal schools, which were established in order to provide at least one female teacher-training school in each prefecture. Higher education for women was not considered essential for producing good wives and wise mothers. Thus, the establishment of private higher educational institutes for women by individuals such as Naruse was incompatible with the national policy regarding women's education. Various criticisms were focused on Naruse's university before and after its opening. It was considered premature by some. An objection to women's higher education was even raised among the guests at the ceremony for the foundation of Japan Women's University, at which a heated discussion took place on the topic.

Naruse's educational policy at Japan Women's University was based on his ideals as outlined in *Joshi Kyoiku* (*Women's Education*). They can be summarized by these principles: true conviction, creativity, and cooperation and service. True conviction was the basis of his policy. It was anchored in the concept of self-conviction attained through character education. Although Naruse acquired his view of character through his belief in Christianity, a result of studying in the United States, it developed into a pantheistic view of character. He explained that "the concept of character is ascribed to all human activities and is the source of values on all aspects of life. We are developed out of the spirit of the universe. Human beings are valued for the manifestation in them of the infinite life." Ultimately, Naruse considered Christ to be the model of the spirit of the universe.

Naruse tried to foster conviction toward character building and aimed at the cultivation of independent character through weekly lectures on practical ethics, assigning theses on the topic of beliefs. He conducted many activities in the school dormitory at Karuizawa during the summer and in the Shuyokan (Hall of Mental Training) on the university campus to reinforce his concepts. Religious education was given great importance in the formation of character. Students were expected to participate in religious activities within an established religion through personal meditation and to engage in other spiritual activities. The process was entrusted to individual judgment.

Creativity involved seeking one's individual endowments and developing them. Through intellectual study, creativity could be cultivated. In those days intellectual training for girls was commonly thought of as something that weakened girls' health. Naruse's promotion of women's creative education thus was undertaken under difficult circumstances. Naruse's views on creative self-expression should be considered. In 1907 he talked at length about the importance of self-expression and then insisted upon *"shogyo*-ism," his interpretation of pragmatism. Pragmatic education forced students to confront their environment, and through it, he thought, the spirit of independence could be heightened, leading to an even higher creative search for truth.

Accordingly, Naruse invited many scholars both from Japan and abroad to give lectures to the students. The Japan Women's University also provided many elective subjects, such as home economics and literature, so that students would not be restricted only to their majors, in order to give them a variety of opportunities to think, study, and be challenged. The encouragement of colloquiums, exhibitions, literary society activities, sports, and student councils were all manifestations of the policy of encouraging students in self-improvement.

Cooperation and service can be effected on the basis of the preceding principles. The social relationship of mankind was interpreted as the "relationship between spirit and character in which many people can share common experiences. Such a relationship can broaden one's horizons, strengthen individual character, and enrich one's experiences." He explained that "the thorough development of one's social nature is indispensable not only for individual development and the complete formation of character but also for the stabilization of social unity." Because Naruse thought that socialization was not only theory but practice, he believed that "it is essential that the individual have an interest in life and acquire the ability to develop a social life, rather than merely understand theoretically its necessity and values."

Naruse encouraged students to participate in self-government. He believed that students' autonomous activities should be conducted with responsibility and without interference from the administration and faculty. In the latter half of each academic year, the student government held a series of meetings to determine the goals for the following year. The annual schedule of activities was then drawn up by the student government but turned over to the students in charge of each class level for implementation. The student organization was responsible not only for routine student activities but also for the major school events of the year. It also included a circle for shūyōkai (character guidance). Self-governing activities were intended to strengthen the individual's ability to adjust to various circumstances and to deepen the understanding of the division between labor and cooperative work. Newly enrolled students were often bewildered by their new responsibility, since student self-government was unique and a complete contrast with the type of public-school education that emphasized the development of good wives and mothers. A follow-up survey of Japan Women's University graduates reveals that such self-governing activities had a great influence on their lives.

Dormitory life also contributed to the promotion of Naruse's concept of cooperation and service. Several small dormitories, each accommodating twenty to thirty students, were built on campus. Each dormitory had a senior student who acted as a housemother and managed dormitory life under the direction of a dormitory superintendent. As regulations were not severely restrictive on the whole, and daily duties varied, each dormitory developed its own distinct characteristics in management and lifestyle. Every student was in turn placed in charge of some duty in order to experience various activities in running the dormitory. Students also became involved in the purchase and sale of household items with the establishment of a dormitory cooperative.

Students and graduates were also expected to participate in a university extension movement. In 1908–9, when the university was founded, Naruse declared that it should be opened to society.

The extension of a women's university had political, national, economic, and social aspects. He described the role of the extension program with respect to three areas: (1) the educational element—an off-campus extension course, a library service including a mobile library unit, a summer seminar, a correspondence course, and public-welfare work; (2) the economic element—a cooperative movement involving production and distribution of products; and (3) the spiritual element—activities involving moral and aesthetic appreciation. Thus Naruse placed a high value on the tasks the university could undertake beyond the campus.

In the chapter in his book on public-welfare work, Naruse insisted: "It is an urgent business of the university to build small welfare centers organized by students. Accordingly the students would live among the workers and the poor to inspire them with an inner progressive spirit and to improve their lives and increase their happiness." He cited Toynbee Hall, Oxford House, Cambridge House, Blackfriar House, and Hull House as examples of centers for welfare work in other countries.

The idea of university extension in modern Japan was first introduced from the West during the Meiji era but developed primarily during the period of Taisho Democracy from 1918. It should be noted that Naruse's promotion of university extension at an even earlier period was particularly unique since it was designed for women. In addition, the alumni association Ohryukai was organized on a nationwide basis consisting of regional groups in which many alumni actively served to improve local family life, an outgrowth of the extension principle.

Many other activities were also organized under Naruse. For example, in 1908 the correspondence course Joshi Daigaku Kogi (Lectures for Women's Universities) was started; in 1910 a night school was opened; and in 1913 a settlement house operating as a day nursery was opened in Koishikawa, Tokyo. The nature of these activities was described in the gazette *Katei Shuho* (*Home Weekly*), published from June 1904. This publication by the women themselves was in itself a notable achievement at a time when there were very few women with experience in journalism.

Besides his work with Japan Women's University, Naruse contributed to the advancement of women's education by various other activities, notably through publications. With the founding of Japan Women's University, which attracted much public attention, Naruse had many occasions to be interviewed and to express his opinion in public. He published books such as *Shinpo to Kyoiku* (*Progress and Education*) in 1911, *Shin Jidai no Kyoiku* (*Education in the New Era*) in 1914, and *Shin Fujin Kun* (*The New Precepts for Women*) in 1916. He also published numerous pamphlets and the English journal *Life*, later changed to *Life and Light*, for language education.

Another of Naruse's many activities was the organization of Maigetsukai (Monthly Meetings) in 1906 to cope with the problems of women's higher education in the aftermath of the Russo-Japanese War. More than thirty members who were concerned with various aspects of women's education, such as a principal for a women's higher school in Tokyo, gathered to discuss and study not only women's education but also educational problems in general.

In 1912 Kiitsu Kyokai (the Concordia Association) was organized. As mentioned previously, from his pantheistic view of the universe Naruse held the idea that all religions would finally be united in harmony. Based on this point of view, he planned to organize an international movement for the solidarity of the spirit on the eve of World War I because of his deep concern about world tensions. His idea met with the approval of about ten contemporary leaders from various fields, who included Shibusawa Eiichi, Inoue Tetsujiro, Nakajima Rikizo, Ukita Kazutami, Ueda Bin, Anezaki Masaharu, and Sydney Guluck. In August 1914 he traveled to the United States and then to Europe to visit educators, scholars, industrialists, and members of the clergy from each country. With the approval of about 170 persons for the plan to establish the Concordia Association, he returned home to promote the movement in Japan.

Naruse's achievements as a member of the Advisory Board on Education to the government should also be mentioned. This advisory panel was responsible at the time for planning educational reforms stimulated by the rising demand for higher education influenced by the so-called era of Taisho Democracy. Naruse's proposal to reform universities drew much attention within the Board because it placed much importance on "bourgeois democracy," which recognized a higher status of women's universities. However, this plan faced opposition from both the Upper House and the Privy Council. The Board was replaced by the Rinji Kyōiku Kaigi (Provisional Council for Education) in 1917. Naruse was also appointed a member of this council, where he distributed his "*Joshi Kyoiku Kaizen Iken*" (Suggestions for Improving Women's Education). His opinion, however, was too far ahead of the times in so many ways that it had little influence on the report to the government.

The last remarkable event in Naruse's life was the farewell lecture he gave shortly before his death. In the autumn of 1918, Naruse began experiencing internal pain. At the beginning of the new year he learned that he had a terminal case of liver cancer. On January 29 he delivered his last lecture from his bed, entitled "To My Successors," before 1,250 people concerned with education. In his lecture he spoke of the future of women's education and of his state of mind before death: "My true body is the spirit in it. Therefore, the spirit is my character. Although my flesh will decay, my spirit, having been nurtured for over sixty years, will never perish. I feel no anxiety. . ."

This farewell lecture demonstrated that Naruse was a man of profound insights and enlightened thinking and a great educator in the highest sense. One of the graduates who attended the lecture expressed her feelings accordingly:

> He is prepared to face approaching death with calm resignation because he has sacrificed himself totally for his life's work. His absolute determination to live up to his principles to work for others to the end strikes us as being his greatest asset. While we listened to him on that memorable afternoon we felt that we somehow became spiritualized, rising above the bitterness of sorrow and death; yet, at the same time he made us realize the profound meaning of our own existence.

Naruse's spirit of education was given life in Japan Women's University. He inspired and encouraged those who promoted women's education with his lifetime devoted to the founding of a women's higher educational institution. However, the foundation of his school was not the only matter that ranked high in his mind. In the diary he kept during his first stay in the United States, he wrote: "My purpose is to pursue my calling to promote the status of women; to grant them virtue; to give them power, knowledge, and discipline; to help them create an 'ideal home'; to build their character; to enrich their lives in order for them to enrich others by saving people from disease and poverty; and to help them create an ideal society." In his life he always strove for the ideal, which attracted many people. His educational ideal was independence of governmental authority, making it possible for him to develop his thought freely from a universal point of view. It is for these reasons that Naruse's thought and practice remain appealing.

The Life of Naruse Jinzo

1858	Born of a samurai family in Yamaguchi Prefecture.
1876	Graduated from the Kiyoshi Teacher's Training School.
1877	Baptized a Christian at the Naniwa Church in Osaka.
1878	Became a teacher at Baika Women's School.
1881	Published *The Duties of Women.*
1882	Ordained as a Christian minister.
1886	Became a pastor at the Niigata Church; established the Niigata Girl's School.
1890	Traveled to the United States to attend courses at the Andover Theological Seminary and Clark University; published *Modern Paul.*
1894	Returned to Japan; appointed principal, Baika Girls' School.
1896	Published *Women's Education.* Resigned the principalship at Baika Girls' School and launched a movement to establish a new college for women.
1901	Founded Japan Women's University (Nihon Joshi Daigaku).
1906	Established a primary school attached to Japan Women's University.
1911	Published *Progress and Education.*

1912   Organized the Concordia Association.
1914   Traveled to Europe and North America; published *Education for the New Era.*
1916   Published *The New Precepts for Women.*
1919   Wrote *Three Essential Points*; died on March 4.

About the Author

Kuni Nakajima was born in Tokyo in 1929, and graduated from Japan Women's University in 1948. After graduate study at Tokyo Bunrika University, she joined the faculty of Japan Women's University, where she is now Professor. Her publications (in Japanese) include *Women's Education in Japan* (1965) and (as Editor) *The Works of Naruse Jinzo.*

Uchimura Kanzo in 1923.

Uchimura Kanzo

[1861-1930]

Kiyoko Takeda Cho

Uchimura Kanzo often described himself as a Japanese, the son of a samurai, and an independent Christian. In reality he was one of the leading intellectuals and Christian educators in Japanese cultural history. He was uniquely the creation of his times, a fiercely independent man of vision with a deep sense of spiritual conviction. As founder of Mukyokai, the "non-church" indigenous Christian movement in Japan, Uchimura became an evangelist outside established churches with their missionaries. He also courageously criticized the absolutist ideology of his country, calling for a nation of justice and dignity of the human spirit.

Uchimura became a convinced pacifist during the Russo-Japanese War at the turn of the century, commenting that "war is worse than any human vice." Previously, at the time of the Sino-Japanese War (1894–95), he had written about the Japanese "victory" leading to the annexation of Korea in an essay entitled "Justification of the Korea War," which he sent to his friends abroad. However, he became convinced that the war and its booty had had a pernicious influence on the life and ethics of the Japanese people; he had already become a resolute pacifist by the time war was declared between Japan and Russia in 1904, and he published many antiwar statements protesting Japan's involvement.

Uchimura was converted to Christianity in 1878 as a student at the Sapporo College of Agriculture (presently Hokkaido University), under the indirect but lasting influence of William S. Clark (1826–68). The well-known American educator, President of the Massachusetts State University of Agriculture, had been invited to Japan to participate in the launching of a new college of agriculture. Dr. Clark had already left for home by the time Uchimura enrolled in the newly formed institution. Nevertheless the distinguished American educator's influence on the students continued long after his departure. Such notable classmates as Nitobe Inazo and Miyabe Kingo, among a host of others, represented a new vanguard of intellectuals who made vital contributions to the development of modern Japan.

Uchimura was later to adopt an evangelical orthodox form of Christianity, with emphasis on atonement, under the personal influence of Julius Hawley Seelye (1824–95), president of Amherst College in Massachusetts. His Christian faith, however, was not merely a cultural imitation of western Christianity. Rather, as a "samurai Christian," he endeavored to fuse Christian beliefs with elements of Japanese culture. From his Christian convictions, however, he could not rationalize such components of Japanese society as emperor-worship, ultranationalism, and patriotism that led to imperialistic aggression; hence his often severe criticism of contemporary society.

In one of his most famous books, *How I Became a Christian* (1895), he also expressed disappointment with the Christian land—the United States—where he arrived in 1885 with deep admiration as well as unrealistic expectations:

> My idea of Christian America was lofty, religious, puritanic. I dreamed of its templed hills, and rocks that rang with hymns and praises. . . . Indeed, the image of America as pictured upon my mind was that of a Holy Land.

Like his fellow Japanese travelers, Uchimura did not fail to recognize the ambiguities and evils of American society, such as crime and abusive racial prejudice against native Indians, the descendants of slaves, and Chinese immigrants who persisted in their traditional lifestyle in the new land. This visitor from Japan, coming from a so-called backward, heathen oriental land, slowly became aware of the indigenous virtues of his homeland, some of a very simple nature and taken as a matter of course, which he realized ought to be cherished:

Uchimura as a student at Amherst College, Massachusetts, in 1887.

A family picture, 1910.

Indeed, insecurity of things in Christendom is something to which we were wholly unaccustomed. Never have I seen more extensive use of keys than among these Christian people. We in our heathen homes have but little course to keys. Our houses, most of them, are open to everybody. Cats come in and out at their own sweet pleasure, and men go to siesta in their beds with zephyrs blowing over their faces; and no apprehensions are felt of our servants or neighbors ever transgressing upon our possessions. But things are quite otherwise in Christendom.

During his three-and-a-half-year stay in the United States, Uchimura was hospitably treated, and he developed several close friendships. He gradually became aware of the impact of Christianity on the spiritual and moral life of the American people, subsequently concluding that "if Christendom's evils are so evil, how virtuous are its virtues." He discovered Christianity in an old couple who lived quietly at the edge of the city as well as in great figures such as the president of the United States. He became resolutely convinced of the necessity for Christianity in the world:

Yes, Christianity we do need. We need it not so much to demolish our idols of wood and stone. Those are innocent things compared with other idols worshipped in Heathendom and elsewhere. We need it to make our bad appear worse, and our good appear better. It only can convince us of sin; and convincing us of it, can help us to rise above it, and conquer it. Heathenism I always consider as a tepid state of human existence; . . . it is neither very warm nor very cold. A lethargic life is a weak life. It feels pain less, hence rejoices less. *De profundis* is not of heathenism. We need Christianity to intensify us; to swear fealty to our God, and enmity toward Devils. . . . Christianity is getting to be a necessity with all of us.

Based on his experiences in America and his deep faith in Christianity as a result of it, he nevertheless expressed his consciousness of being a foreigner in a foreign land: "Three-and-a-half years' stay in it, with the best of hospitality it gave me, and the closest of friendships I formed in it, did not entirely naturalize me to it. I remained a stranger throughout, and I never had exerted myself to be otherwise."

Uchimura's autobiography *How I Became a Christian* dramatically reveals the process of Uchimura's transformation. He describes the fusion in his thought of the two great influences, Japan and Christianity:

> I love two J's and no third: one is Jesus, and the other is Japan. I do not know which I love more, Jesus or Japan. I am hated by my countrymen for Jesus' sake as '*yaso*,' and I am disliked by foreign missionaries for Japan's sake as national and narrow. No matter; I may lose all my friends, but I cannot lose Jesus and Japan. . . . and Japan clarifies and objectivises my love for Jesus.

Upon his rturn home, Uchimura became a teacher who considered it his challenge to bring about a national regeneration in the conscience and character of the Japanese by revitalizing the spirit of the country. He did not presumptuously set out to supplant the traditional value system of Japan with Christian beliefs or modern western thought; neither, however, did he attempt to preserve the traditional Japanese way of thinking. His approach to developing a new modern spirit and character of the Japanese people was expressed symbolically in his words: "To graft the Christian gospel onto the trunk of Bushido." By this he meant implanting the message of Christianity into the potentially receptive elements embodied in the traditional Japanese spiritual soil, and thus to create a modern spirit and ethos for a new Japan.

In 1891 the Imperial Rescript on Education, embodying the basic principles of state-centered and -controlled Japanese education, was promulgated by the Meiji government. During the ceremony of receipt of the Rescript at the First High School, where Uchimura was serving as a part-time teacher, he failed to pay homage by refusing to join the others in bowing before the sacred document. The incident was promptly labeled "lèse-majesté," and Uchimura came under heavy criticism from many nationalists. Among the severest critics was Professor Inoue Tetsujiro of the prestigious Tokyo Imperial University, who contemptuously attacked Uchimura and Japanese Christians in general as enemies of the state and of the Emperor. He charged them with violating an unwritten moral code of conduct by treating Japanese and foreigners with equal regard.

This widely publicized event developed into a nationwide controversy of considerable historical significance in modern Japan, engulfing many Christians, Buddhists, and nationalists in the ensuing dispute. Uchimura, branded a traitor, was summarily removed from his teaching post and virtually ostracized from society. In retrospect, the incident represented an ideological maneuver by ultranationalists to silence liberals, democrats, and other progressives, using Christians as scapegoats.

In spite of Uchimura's patriotic zeal, common among Japanese of samurai background, he found himself treated as a traitor in his own country. This bitter, lonely experience led him to reexamine the nature of his patriotism and motivated him to write one of his most famous books, *Japan and the Japanese* (1894), later renamed *Representative Men of Japan*. In this book he selected five Japanese figures whose personal qualities exhibited the noble universal values within Japanese cultural tradition to which Uchimura's Christian faith would be grafted. We are able to gain a better understanding of his thinking by looking at the individuals he chose to write about.

The first was Saigo Takamori, one of the leaders of the new Japan and the last samurai statesman. As a scholar of the Wang Yang-ming school, he cherished moral values above all else. Uchimura believed that Wang Yang-ming's was a progressive philosophy, full of promise, whose similiarities to Christianity had been previously recognized by others. Saigo, a leader of the Meiji Restoration, who later turned against the central government and died in 1877 in the abortive Satsuma rebellion, wrote the following words, which Uchimura concluded "he heard . . . directly from Heaven":

He that follows the heavenly way abases not himself even though the whole world speaks evil of him; neither thinks he himself sufficient even though they in unison praise his name. . . . Deal with Heaven, and never with men. Do all things for Heaven's sake. Blame not others; only search into the lack of sincerity in us. The law is of the universe and is natural. Hence, he only can keep it who makes it his aim to fear and serve Heaven. . . . Heaven loves all men alike. So we must love others with the love with which we love ourselves.

The second figure admired by Uchimura was Uesugi Yozen, a feudal lord who carried out social reforms among his clan so that no one would live on another's labor. During periods of peace, Uesugi transformed his samurai warriors into farmers, reclaiming thousands of acres of wilderness to productive uses. All samurai families were also required to plant around their homes seedlings of cash crops; the more than one million seedlings planted brought considerable economic prosperity to the clan as a whole. Uchimura, in response, wrote: "One beautiful feature of Oriental knowledge is that it has never treated economy apart from morality. Wealth with their philosophers is always the effect of virtue, and the two bear the same relationship to each other that the fruit bears to the tree."

The third character is Ninomiya Sontoku, an agricultural technologist and philosopher who taught poor farmers to become productive by developing wastelands into fertile farmland. This most difficult task was accomplished with the aid of moral teachings that transformed farmers' attitudes toward life.

The fourth distinguished Japanese chosen by Uchimura was Nichiren, the Buddhist priest known to all Japanese, who founded one of the major sects of Buddhism and who courageously stood up to persecution by political leaders.

In describing the life of the fifth and last admired person, Nakae Toju, a local village educator, Uchimura used the opportunity to express his own thoughts on education. "Teaching in Old Japan," the chapter on Nakae, reveals Uchimura's responses to his experiences in the West by reflecting on the significance of education in old Japan under the influence of such native teachers as Nakae:

"What kind of schooling had you in Japan before we westerners came to save you? You Japanese seem to be the cleverest set of people among heathens, and you must have had some training, moral and intellectual, to make you what you have been and are.

Such are the questions, and oftentimes their tone, put to us by some civilized westerners, when some of us appeared in their midst, fresh from our country. To which our answer has been somewhat as follows:

Yes, we had schooling, and considerable of it. We believe, at least, eight out of the Ten Commandments we learnt from the lips of our fathers while in our mother's laps. We knew that might is not right, that the universe does not stand upon selfishness, that stealing is not right in whatever form it appears, that life and property are not after all the things we should aim at, and many other things. We had schools, too, and teachers, quite different from what we see in your great West and now imitated in our land. First of all, we never have thought of schools as shops for intellectual apprenticeship. We were sent there not so much for earning a livelihood when we had finished with them, as for becoming true men—*kunshi*, as we called them, akin to gentlemen in England.

Uchimura claimed that earlier Japanese teachers such as Nakae had much in common with great western philosophers like Socrates and Plato in their approach to education. He pointed out the traditional close relations between teacher and student— the *sensei* (master) and *deshi* (disciple) relationship, of deep personal respect and commitment in historical Japanese interpersonal ties—as examples. He recognized in this profound similarities to the relationship of Jesus and his disciples, in the parable of the good shepherd and his sheep found in the Bible.

In his own way, Uchimura thus endeavored to search for humanitarian values in traditional Japanese education in order to bridge them with universal or Christian values. Nakae was a prime example. His external poverty and simplicity were out of proportion to his internal integrity and abundant wealth. Although Nakae was brought up in the conservative Chu philosophy, he was deeply influenced at a later stage by the progressive Chinese Wang Yang-ming.

Uchimura himself was impressed with Wang Yang-ming's philosophy, which, he believed, had not produced timid, fearful, conservative people like the majority of Japanese, but had developed the progressive side of Confucianism. Nakae drew strength from this teaching, which helped him better understand Confucius. The teachings of this venerable oriental sage helped to make Nakae a practical man as well as a great village educator.

Under Nakae's personal influence, the villagers came to recognize the importance of such human virtues as honesty, justice, and sincerity. Many feudal lords invited Nakae to come to their area to spread his positive influence among their retainers, but he refused, preferring to teach the local village children. Once, when a feudal lord came to invite him to join his clan, Nakae forced the visiting ruler to wait in front of the school gate until he finished the lessons. Education was more important to him than the visiting dignitary. Such was the attitude of an early village teacher in Japan that appealed to Uchimura.

In Uchimura's *Representative Men of Japan*, we encounter his interesting methodology in transforming traditional value systems of Japan. On the one hand he proclaims the discontinuity of some traditionalistic negative elements. On the other he carefully selects certain promising elements from the depth of traditional thought and morality that can be developed and linked to universal values. Thus he carefully leads both Japanese and westerners in discovering clues in the continuity and discontinuity of the traditional value system.

Through Uchimura's five representative figures from Japan, he also reveals his system of thought for the modernization of Japan based on the following principals: a political leadership that respects justice beyond personal interest; social reform that renders the people productive without exploiting others; agricultural reform based upon morality, honesty, and diligence; education that respects the individual; and religious dignity before the political powers of the day.

Uchimura was a Christian evangelist. He was also a distinguished educator who played a historical role by greatly influencing the people of his day in transforming their value systems and consciousness in the formation of a new Japanese character. He was instrumental in the process of preserving positive values from the old Japan while ushering in an era of the new Japan. As a Christian he valiantly endeavored to show the relevance of Christianity in the transformation. In the preface to the German edition of *Representative Men of Japan*, he explains his broad historical approach to renewal:

> I want to thank God that we did not come into existence as barbarians. Before I was conceived in my mother's womb, various influences formed me. For two thousand years, preparation was made before I was chosen to be a Christian. As a nation as well as an individual, conversion cannot be done in a day. Conversion in the true sense is an enterprise of several centuries.

Although he was not an educator in the sense of a schoolteacher, Uchimura's influence on Japanese education was profound from the middle Meiji to the early Showa years (1890–1930). During these many years he published a large number of highly influential books, including *The Comfort of Christians* (1893), *Representative Men of Japan* (1894), *How I Became a Christian* (1895), and *Relics to the Later Generations* (1894). Several of these publications were translated into many other languages.

He was associated with the periodicals *The Tokyo Independent Magazine* (1890–1900), *Study of the Bible* (1900–1903), *Mukyokai* (*The Non-Church Movement*, 1901–1902), and was also known for his antiwar essays, carried in the popular newspaper *Yorozu Choho*. Through his prolific writings, Uchimura reached enthusiastic readers from all over Japan. Among them were intellectuals, people of various professions, and many housewives. Consequently his influence on society was deep-rooted.

One of Uchimura's most enduring educational contributions resulted from his small study groups. One of these, the Kashiwakai, was formed in 1909 with a dozen students from the prestigious First High School who were assembled by the school's principal, Nitobe Inazo. Among these students were Takagi Yasaka, later to become a well-known legal scholar; Maeda Tamon and Morito Tatsuo, who would become postwar ministers of education;

Iwanaga Yukichi, who founded the Kyodo News Service; Fujii Takeshi, Tsukamoto Torajiro, and Kurosaki Koichi, who would be leaders of the Christian Mukyokai movement; and Sawada Renzo, ambassador to the United Nations. About ten years later the name of the group was changed to Emmaus-kai, with new members such as Yanaihara Tadao, a future president of the University of Tokyo; Mitani Takanobu, who would become ambassador to France; and Kanazawa Tsuneo, a well-known Mukyokai leader, joining the select group.

Another study group, called the Hakuukai, was formed in 1911, also with students mainly from Nitobe's First High School. Among its notable members were Nambara Shigeru, who was to be President of the University of Tokyo and chairman of the Council on Educational Reform during the American Occupation; Sakata Tasuku, later President of Kwanto Gakuin; and Nagayo Yoshiro, the author of *Twenty-six Martyrs*. These outstanding leaders of modern Japan possessed a unique spiritual quality that was nurtured under the guidance of two of Japan's greatest educators, Uchimura and Nitobe. One of the most significant influences of these various study groups was in the character-building of the young participants who were destined to become leaders of modern Japan.

Dr. Yanaihara, expelled from his position as professor of economics at the University of Tokyo by the wartime militarists, only to become president of the same institution after the war, explained how Uchimura and Nitobe recognized their differences. Dr. Nitobe, the consummate educator, was asked how his Christian faith differed from that of Uchimura. His answer: "Uchimura's faith is that of the front gate, while mine is that of the side gate, which means a gate of sorrows." By this he meant that Uchimura, as an orthodox Christian, confronted believers and unbelievers with the righteousness of God and claimed repentance for their sins. He was more like a stern father to his youthful followers. Nitobe, on the other hand, was a Quaker whose noble qualities epitomized tolerance. He was kind and generous to all, with a nurturing personality.

These two great educators, whose destinies were intertwined, had been good friends ever since their student days together at the Sapporo College of Agriculture. They knew well each other's strengths and weaknesses. Nitobe sent carefully selected students trained in liberal education at his prestigious First National Higher School to experience the more severe personality and the teach ings of Christianity under Uchimura prior to their entrance to Tokyo Imperial University. Uchimura welcomed these promising students chosen by the renowned Nitobe, calling them in jest "the eggs of vipers." These young men, under the guidance of these two contrasting figures, not only developed into brilliant scholars; they became men of strong spirit who courageously resisted ul- tranationalism during wartime and assumed leadership in the democratic reforms of Japanese education after the war.

Uchimura had been educated as a natural scientist at the Sapporo College of Agriculture. With this educational back- ground and his keen analytical insight, he was uniquely suited to deal with questions of religion and science that had become the center of a raging controversy at that time. During the Meiji period, Charles Darwin's theory of evolution was introduced into Japan and soon became the determining influence in aca- demic theories not only in natural science but in virtually all disciplines including social science and philosophy. Darwinism became the "almighty science," rendering all religions, including Christianity, merely superstitious beliefs.

The most notable application of Darwinism to social science was undertaken by Kato Hiroyuki, Professor of Law and Presi- dent of Tokyo Imperial University, who had adopted the theory of social Darwinism as developed in Germany. Kato employed this theory in defense of nationalism, arguing that a nation rep- resented the organic whole and its citizens were its hands and feet. He posited the Emperor as the head of the nation as it strug- gled for existence in the context of the survival of the fittest. Kato utilized Darwinian theory to battle the popular Freedom and Human Rights movement in the name of science. He attacked Christianity as being detrimental to Japan because its loyalty went beyond the nation.

As a Christian and a natural scientist, Uchimura blended Christian faith and Darwinian theory. In fact, he claimed that the three books that had the greatest impact on his life were the Bible, the biography of Oliver Cromwell, and Darwin's *Origin of Species.* Through the Bible he learned that God governs the conscience of human beings, liberating them from worldly authority. Through the life of Oliver Cromwell, leader of the Puritan Revolution in England, he came to understand the principles of political democracy and how to devote oneself to the pursuit of truth.

Darwinism taught Uchimura how to understand the universe. To him, evolution explained the way God created and sustains it. He thought that science could not develop in Japan because the human mind was suppressed there. Only when the mind is free to surpass nature and seeks to investigate it thoroughly, he said, can science emerge; consequently, there is a deep relation between monotheistic faith and science. Uchimura wrote that there were two types of evolution: atheistic and theistic. For him, science and religion were on different levels. He attempted to clarify the relationship between the plane of Christianity and that of natural science, between religious truth and scientific truth.

The contribution made by Uchimura may be measured not only by the prominent role he played in the education of many outstanding national leaders. Throughout his life he energetically traveled the length and breadth of Japan, visiting his followers, preaching, and encouraging them to keep the faith. He never wavered in this mission. In Hokkaido, for example, where Uchimura studied, there were as a consequence active Christians among farmers, postal workers, tailors, barbers, and people from all walks of life.

An example of how his influence was spread through his followers can be understood by the case of Iguchi Kigenji from rural Nagano Prefecture. Iguchi, inspired by Uchimura and supported by fellow Christian farmers of the area, founded Kensei Gijuku, one of the smallest schools in all of Japan, at the foot of the Japan Alps. He was determined to teach the children of local farmers, who, in spite of their eagerness to learn, could not enter the high school because of financial difficulties.

Iguchi expressed the basic educational principle of his new school in these words: "Our school is like a family. We try to develop the character of each student with lasting spiritual and cultural qualities; to integrate the traditional oriental values with western Christian humanitarian values; and to produce individuals who would contribute to the welfare of the society and mankind."

In 1901 Uchimura visited this tiny school and later wrote about his impressions: "I love nature. I particularly love mountains. Wherever there are mountains, there are rocks. Wherever there are rocks, there are men of spirit like rocks."

Not only did Uchimura visit his school from time to time, but Iguchi sent some of his most promising students to Uchimura during the agricultural off-season to receive his personal guidance. Uchimura claimed that even though Iguchi's school may have been the smallest in Japan, it was the most precious. He likened Iguchi to one of the great European educators, calling him the Pestalozzi of Japan. On December 1, 1923, the thirtieth anniversary of the school, Uchimura sent his greetings on the occasion:

> Mr. Iguchi has given an answer to the question, what is education. Education is not school buildings. Education can be done when one teacher faces one student with deep respect and trust. . . . The purpose of education is first of all to develop human personality. Pestalozzi was a great educator exactly in this meaning. . . . Mr. Iguchi's educational effort of the past thirty years bears that meaning. I dare to say in his educational effort we find an image of the Pestalozzian spirit. . . . Great work cannot be completed within one generation. Mr. Iguchi and Kensei Gijuku have demonstrated a precious and meaningful experiment of education in modern Japan. Future generations will learn humbly about the true meaning of human education from his experiment.

Nearly 800 local youths passed through Iguchi's school, most of them becoming farmers, and not a few stimulated with a sense of service to the society. Some of these graduates of this unusual school distinguished themselves. For example, Kiyosawa Kiyoshi later emigrated to the United States, working his way through college. He eventually became a well-known journalist and a diplomatic critic who courageously criticized the ultranationalists during the war. Another graduate, Ogiwara Rokuzan, a famous sculptor, studied art in America and France, coming under the influence of Rodin. Ogiwara was one of the pioneers of modern art in Japan. Such were a few of the products of the mountain school run by "Japan's Pestalozzi," who received inspiration and continual support from Uchimura.

Uchimura Kanzo was not known as a temperate individual. Indeed, his personality was strong. His less idealistic side was criticized as quarrelsome and contentious. His actions were characteristically forthright. A good example was his provocative refusal to bow before the Imperial Rescript on Education, which nevertheless became a critical opportunity for Christians and the public at large to ponder the issues of freedom and individual dignity in a nation where nationalism was glorified. When Uchimura was hired to teach at a mission school in Niigata Prefecture, he impetuously insisted on teaching about Buddhism, which the local missionaries opposed. After a confrontation, he resigned.

Arishima Takeo, a popular literary writer, was a student of both Uchimura and Nitobe. Uchimura fully intended that Arishima would become his successor as leader of the Mukyokai movement. However, Arishima declared himself an apostate because he could not be reconciled with Uchimura's stern and ascetic Christianity.

Another figure, Masamune Hakucho, a literary critic, had deep respect for Uchimura's literary insight and ability to grasp the depths of human problems. But he, too, could not reconcile himself to Uchimura's Spartan discipline. He particularly could not accept Uchimura's intolerance of the enjoyment of drama, music, or literature. Masamune concluded that such a Christian is a distorted being, unable to appreciate the beauty of art or literature. He severed his allegiance to Uchimura by writing that "Uchimura's affection and hatred are both unusually strong. He has an exceptional insight into the depths of human nature. If he had been a literary man, he would have been a truly great figure. He was, however, poisoned by Christianity."

Other distinguished people who experienced Uchimura's wrath included Tanaka Kotaro, professor of law at Tokyo Imperial University, minister of education in postwar Japan, and later a judge at the International Court of Justice in the Hague. He converted to Catholicism because Uchimura expelled him from the group. Tsukamoto Torajiro, one of Uchimura's closest disciples, who succeeded him as the moving spirit of Mukyokai, ultimately broke with his leader, taking with him a large number of followers. Uchimura declared: "It is a cleanup of the members. I am not a Mukyokai member, which is fashionable today." By this time he had reached the age of sixty-eight and was failing in health, suffering the fate of a once great leader who tenaciously held firm to his convictions under trying circumstances to the end. The following year, 1930, he died in loneliness.

Uchimura was not a generous or gentle educator. Often he placed obstacles before his students and followers as well as his critics. Indeed, he made a deep impact upon others through the reverberations of those very obstacles. In this sense he was a unique character who played a catalytic role in modern Japan. His influence lives on in his homeland, not only among Christians but also among others who are challenged by him. The issues that confronted him in his day concerning the sinfulness of man and of nations are still challenging us. He summed up his belief in a few short lines appropriately inscribed on his tombstone:

> I for Japan
> Japan for the World
> The World for Christ
> And all for God.

The Life of Uchimura Kanzo

1861	Born into a samurai family in Edo (Tokyo).
1877	Entered Sapporo Agricultural College with Nitobe Inazo.
1878	Baptized by M. C. Harris.
1881	Graduated from the Agricultural College and hired by the Hokkaido Development Bureau.
1882	Established Sapporo Independent Church.
1885	Went to the United States, initially working at a mental

asylum for six months before entering Amherst College, Massachusetts, as a special student.

1886 Experienced born-again conversion under the influence of Amherst President Julius Hawley Seelye.

1887 Graduated from Amherst and entered Hartford Theological Seminary.

1888 Returned to Japan; hired by Hokuetsu Gakkan School in Niigata as head teacher; resigned.

1890 Appointed part-time lecturer at the First National Higher School to teach English.

1891 Refused to bow before the Imperial Rescript on Education at a school ceremony; lost his job.

1894 Published *Japan and the Japanese* (later retitled *Representative Men of Japan*).

1895 Published *How I Became a Christian* in Japan and in the U.S.A.

1901 Inaugurated the Mukyokai (Non-church Christian Movement).

1909 Formed Kashiwa-kai study group.

1926 Launched the English-language magazine *The Japan Christian Intelligencer*.

1930 Died at the age of 69.

About the Author

Kiyoko Takeda Cho was born in 1917 in Hyogo Prefecture. She graduated from Kobe Jogakuin College in 1939, and from Olivet College in the United States in 1941. After studying at Columbia University and Union Theological Seminary, she returned to Japan and received her doctorate from the University of Tokyo in 1961. She joined the faculty of International Christian University in 1953, and retired as Graduate School Professor in 1988. She is the author of many publications in Japanese and, in English, of *The Dual Image of the Japanese Emperor* (1988).

Nitobe Inazo in New York, 1932.

Nitobe Inazo

[1862–1933]

Kiyoko Takeda Cho

Educational philosophy and development in the modern history
of Japan have been deeply influenced by a combination of nationalism and utilitarianism. There have, nevertheless, been
several major progressive movements of historical significance
that encouraged respect for individuality and enhancement of
personality. Among the most critical of these are found in the
precepts of human rights advocated by Fukuzawa Yukichi and
others during the period of the so-called *bunmei kaika*, or cultural
enlightenment, of the late 1800s; the Christian conception of
man embraced by the mission schools founded in the middle
of the Meiji period; the principles of liberal education inspired
during the short-lived era of Taisho Democracy in the early
1920s; and the postwar democratic reforms of education embodied in the Fundamental Law of Education that supplanted
the prewar Imperial Rescript on Education.

Of the many figures who contributed to the various currents
of progressive thought in recent Japanese history, Nitobe Inazo
is justifiably recognized as playing one of the most prominent
roles. A product of the well-known Sapporo Band, one of the
three fountainheads of Protestantism in prewar Japan, he became
the leader of the liberal education movement during the period
referred to as Taisho Democracy or Taisho humanism. At the
same time, Nitobe reflected the indigenous roots of democratic
thought in prewar Japan that undergirded the reformation of
education in postwar Japan. Among those enlightened leaders
who played decisive roles in the democratization of Japanese

education following World War II, an impressive number were Nitobe's former students.

Dr. Nitobe was best known throughout the world as the author of the classic interpretation of the Japanese mentality entitled *Bushido: The Soul of Japan*. Not only was this gentle scholar a prolific writer in both Japanese and English; he achieved distinction as a leading Japanese Christian who contributed greatly to international and intercultural understanding as, in his own description, "a bridge over the Pacific Ocean." His approach in bridging western and oriental culture—that is, Christianity and the Japanese mind—was unique, being closely allied to but somewhat different from syncretism. The personality and insights of this great Japanese educator are a fascinating topic of study within the history of the modernization of Japanese society and education.

Nitobe was a consummate educator who devoted a lifetime to the advancement of liberal and democratic ideas in education at a period in the history of Japan when this pursuit was fraught with difficulties. First of all, he was directly involved in the reformation of higher education in his position as principal of the prestigious First National Higher School, which prepared its students primarily for Tokyo Imperial University, and as professor, initially at Sapporo University (currently Hokkaido University) and later at Kyoto Imperial University and Tokyo Imperial University. At the First National Higher School, his reforms redirected the highly chauvinistic aims of education to reflect a more liberal persuasion seeking a socially conscious graduate. At the university level he became a pioneering figure in the areas of general education and liberal arts.

Nitobe is also well known for his contribution to the progress of women's education in both its purposes and its academic standards. In sharp contrast to the prevailing education that aimed at producing subservient women, he placed paramount importance on the humanity of all people. As the first president of the distinguished Tokyo Women's Christian University and an early ardent supporter of Tsuda Juku College for Women, he served in the vanguard of women's higher education in Japan. In addition he worked actively in the development of several girls' high schools. Under Nitobe's influence, many outstanding

As a student at Bonn University, 1887.

The Sapporo Band, ca. 1928. Nitobe, at far right, is seated next to Uchimura Kanzo.

women educators, such as Tsuda Ume, Yasui Tetsuko, and Kawai Michiko, became prominent figures in the educational world.

Another area of education in which Nitobe made a distinctive contribution was the founding in 1894 of a night school in Sapporo for working youth of both sexes—a type of school that theretofore was nonexistent in Japan. He also became a popular educator among working youth and poorly educated women throughout the country, through his many articles on education in popular magazines at a time when prominent university professors were not disposed to patronize such "low-class" publications. Through these various channels, this liberal educator exhibited an extraordinary influence over a vast range of Japanese, from high school and university students destined for leadership of the nation to the scantly educated working youth and housewives, with his central doctrine of respect for humanity.

In order to appreciate the significance of Nitobe's contribution to Japanese education, we must briefly consider the social and political trends under way in Japan at the turn of the century, when Nitobe first achieved recognition as a prominent educator. One of the most crucial developments of historical consequence was the declaration of the Imperial Rescript on Education, which followed by one year the promulgation of the Meiji Constitution of 1889. The Constitution set the direction of the new government, which was founded on absolutism with authority vested in the Emperor. The Imperial Rescript on Education subsequently laid the basis for an educational policy aimed at creating subjects who were loyal to the Emperor. The famous lèse-majesté incident, in which Uchimura Kanzo was severely criticized for his failure to bow before the Rescript, followed in 1891, setting the tone surrounding the sacred document. It also sparked a bitter controversy that brought into prominence the conflict between education and religion, particularly Christianity, foreshadowing events to follow. Certain nationalists took advantage of the conflict over the Rescript to attack Christianity. Buddhists utilized the opportunity to join in the criticism by denouncing Christian teachings as antithetical to traditional Japanese social ethics such as loyalty and filial piety. They carefully formulated their arguments in the form of denunciations of Christians as enemies of the state. Various groups became aroused and demonstrated their anger by stoning Christian churches.

Kato Hiroyuki, well-known materialist and, at the time, president of Tokyo Imperial University, stridently attacked Christianity in his books, such as *Waga Kokutai to Kirisutokyo* (*Our National Policy and Christianity*), published in 1907. Kato argued that religion renders the individual superstitious, preventing scientific progress, and wrote that Japan's national policy could not permit "rule by two authorities." In other words, he pounced on the opportunity to condemn Japanese Christians who worshiped the "one true God" rather than the Emperor, even though the Emperor "embodies the supreme being." He described how detrimental Christianity was to the state, emphasizing the importance of all Japanese worshiping the Emperor. Since Tokyo Imperial University was highly respected by the public, an attack on Christianity by its president sparked repercussions. For example, many educated Christians faced serious difficulties as schools grew reluctant to employ Christian graduates of teacher-training institutions. Many other instances can be cited of attacks on Christianity and the ensuing prejudice they aroused.

Following the Russo-Japanese War (1904–5), the government initiated a campaign promoting an ethical system designed to inculcate family-state ideology. In contrast, various intellectual, moral, and religious undercurrents originated spontaneously from among the people themselves. Without openly opposing the government's family-state ideology and national moral principles, these popular private movements amalgamated into a moving spirit known as Taisho humanism or Taisho Democracy. Taisho humanism sought to establish an ideological foundation for the concept that human beings are worthy of respect as individuals—a basis quite different from that on which the government-sponsored ethical system was founded.

It was at this time, when the various divergent movements were activated, that Nitobe Inazo's book *Shuyo* (*Moral Training*) became a best-seller exerting much influence on the young people of Japan. The book's purpose was to provide guidance for Japanese youth on life's problems. It dealt with such matters as the purpose of life, self-control, courage, sincerity, politeness, kindness, and sympathy, and included guiding principles to follow in times of both prosperity and adversity. In presenting his ideas, Nitobe used only vocabulary and expressions readily understood by young people living in Japan's rural communities. He employed the same approach in most of his other popular works, such as *Yowatari no Michi* (*The Art of Living*), *Jikeiroku* (*A Record of Self-Vigilance*), and *Ijin Gunzo* (*Great Men*).

One must now turn to Nitobe's religious background and beliefs in order to more fully comprehend his educational thought and deeds. Nitobe was one of the principal figures among a group of students who became Christians while studying at the Sapporo School of Agriculture in the late 1870s under the tutelage of Professor William Clark from Massachusetts. These students formed what came to be widely known as the Sapporo Band. Among them were such notable figures as Uchimura Kanzo, later to become the central figure in the lèse-majesté incident cited previously.

Nitobe, while subsequently studying at Johns Hopkins University (1884–87), became attracted to Quaker beliefs and joined the Monthly Meeting in Baltimore, Maryland. As befit a Quaker, he was a peace-loving person who respected the inner light in every human being, showing kindness to everyone he met. He was almost maternal in his all-embracing warmth and affection. He cherished the special endowments of each of his disciples, lighting a lamp for them to follow in their new way of life. His followers were of every description and from all over Japan, ranging from the well educated to the unschooled. To them, Nitobe was their beloved teacher, and in return they responded with unreserved affection and allegiance.

Nitobe particularly reacted to one precept of Quakerism, namely, that all human beings are endowed with an inner light regardless of their temperament, race, or religion. He was also deeply impressed by the efforts of the Quakers to express in their daily lives the principle of equality. For example, English Quakers never removed their hats whether in the presence of kings or in the midst of the poor. They practiced this principle of equality in their dealings with both men and women, American Indians, and blacks. They strove to propagate education, particularly through improving educational facilities for the poor. Nitobe described these noble qualities with great feeling in his book *A Japanese View of Quakerism*. He concluded: "The equality of men and women, the abolition of slavery, the humane treatment of the insane and the criminal, freedom of speech, liberty of conscience, the general spread of education among the poor, the spiritual interpretation of the Bible—all these are assets to their credit."

He wrote about this theme in his *Ichinichi Ichigen (A Word a Day)*:

> On this same day in the year 1828, Tolstoy, the man who put equality into practice, was born, and on this same day in 1871, the *eta* class [the outcastes of Japan] became full citizens. When you see someone, always think, "He is a man just as I. He therefore also respects his parents, loves his children, wishes to be well spoken of by others, and wants to have money. Whether he is a beggar or a nobleman, a saint or a robber, a human being is a human being, and we should respect each one with the same sympathy we would extend to any other person."

In this simple passage we find Nitobe taking upon his own shoulders the sufferings of others. His faith, which he himself described symbolically as a "side gate" instead of a "front gate," or as a "gate of sorrow," was the foundation for his deep interest in personal encounters with others and for his attempts to help solve their problems. Based on this outlook on human relationships, he displayed a lifelong attitude of tolerance conspicuously devoid of malice.

In his book *Bushido: The Soul of Japan*, which was translated into many languages, Nitobe claimed that *bushido* was the principal driving force behind the construction of a new Japan following the Meiji Restoration. He wrote, "'God has granted,' says the Koran, 'to every people a prophet in its own tongue.' The Seeds of the Kingdom, as vouched for and apprehended by the Japanese mind, blossomed in *bushido*." When the mother institution, feudalism, was gone, *bushido* was left an orphan destined to fade away as "the captains and the kings depart." Nitobe concluded that Christianity would, in a sense, succeed to the spirit of *bushido* and breathe new life into it. Thus, he was seeking to graft Christianity onto a *bushido* trunk, the sources of which he traced to Buddhism, Shintoism, and Confucianism, giving an impression of syncretism in Nitobe's thought.

In his book *Shuyo*, Nitobe gave the following explanation of how critical it is for people to be aware of what he called vertical relationships:

> I would like you to consider the fact that human life does not rest only on horizontal social relationships. If we were to stand only on the horizontal line that constitutes the majority of our social relationships, we might become prominent among the masses of the people, and we might even acquire considerable control over them. But if we advance one step further in our thinking, we will find that our relationships extend beyond those that we have with other men and women. We will see that there is also a vertical relationship to consider. . . . Just think about establishing a relationship with that which is above and beyond humans. Only the individual who is able to establish a vertical relationship will be able, for the first time, to decide upon the basic course his life should take.

This explanation of the existence of the transcendental appears ambiguous and vague. But Nitobe was trying to exemplify how an individual can achieve self-perspective by looking up to, and establishing a relationship with, something that transcends human beings. In his bestseller *Ichinichi Ichigen* Nitobe freely draws lessons for life from Buddhist and Confucian sources, ancient poems, the Imperial Rescript on Education, and the Bible.

Although Nitobe is generally considered to have idealized the code of *bushido* when he introduced the concept to the West through his famous book, that conclusion must be tempered by his actions. At the same time he was sharply critical of the Japanese sense of shame and honor, as well as the traditional patterns of thought. He addressed himself directly to his countrymen by castigating them for their search for fame as the central purpose of life. Nitobe's approach was not simply to criticize the Japanese for their attitudes toward shame and honor, for example. Rather, he attempted to associate these feelings with a consciousness of guilt.

The following episode best illustrates the simple message Nitobe gave to working youth in the countryside as well as to housewives. A friend of his, the eldest son in a family long accustomed to social prestige, suddenly became responsible for the future of the family upon its unexpected bankruptcy. In desperation the poor fellow unsuccessfully attempted suicide. However, he eventually regained control over his life, stabilizing the family prospects in the process. The underlying cause of his intense desperation was based on his complete obsession with the traditional social class distinctions permeating the society, in conformity with which he looked upon all those socially inferior to him with disdain. But when he found himself at the very bottom of the social register, he came to the stark realization of what life is about for those existing with the barest of material goods. The new awareness of the meaning of life drastically altered this individual's image of the unfortunate people in society. By treating all human beings as equals, life gained new meaning and immense satisfaction for him. Before his transformation his principal aspiration in life was to preserve the family heritage, which had been passed down from generation to generation. Having spent his whole life within an isolated environment limited to a few immediate friends and family members at the same social level, this man with his new value system epitomized for Nitobe the conversion all should undergo.

Through such simple teachings, Nitobe strove to transmit a new image governing the attitude and conduct toward human beings among the common people. To him, this social stratum would be most responsive and more likely to actualize the new way of thinking. His goal was to provide guidance for them in overcoming the burdens they were subjected to under the prevailing value system and thereby seek to improve the quality of their lives. Based on these ideals, amid the developing storm of nationalism, Nitobe was gradually introduced into the very mainstream of Japanese education at the turn of the century.

Long before this, however, while only a student himself, Nitobe had already exhibited a keen interest in educational matters. As one example, he envisioned a night school for those deprived individuals unable to benefit from regular schools. In a letter written while studying at Johns Hopkins University in 1885, he first expressed his abiding concern for such a school accordingly:

> It is, indeed, my earnest desire and sincere prayer that I may one day be able to do something for my God and for my country in Sapporo. More than two years ago, while I was still teaching there, I thought strongly of founding a school for the benefit of the people. My idea of Sapporo Academie is that it should accommodate three kinds of pupils: (1) adults to whom lectures should be given in Japanese on History, Economy, Agriculture, and Natural Science; (2) boys and youth who wish to prepare themselves for college or university and yet who cannot regularly attend the *yobikō* [preparatory school]; (3) night school for the rugged children of poor parents, laborers' boys and girls, etc. . . . Never has this idea of education left my mind. Even in buying books here, I always have this object in view.

Two years later, in 1887, he wrote from Bonn University, Germany, that "my favorite dreams for Sapporo are now the establishment of a *yagakkō* [night school] for the poor." Seven years later, in 1894, his dream became a reality when he was finally able to set up a school for the poor in the middle of a run-down section of Sapporo. Nitobe's initial venture into this school for poor working youth involved the cooperation of many people. He used land owned by a local Christian church to begin a rather primitive facility teaching regular school subjects plus vocational courses such as nursing, sewing, and knitting. Students at the Sapporo Agriculture School, Nitobe's home institution, volunteered their services as teachers. He tried to inspire the young students and teachers with his enthusiasm in an effort to render the school a center of enlightenment among the poor of the community.

Growing out of Nitobe's interest in the education of poor working youth were his articles and speeches aimed at them. For example, he published a series of articles on moral training in the popular magazine *Jitsugyo no Nihon* (*Vocational Japan*). In 1911 the series appeared in book form, exerting a strong influence on the thinking of many young Japanese. His other published works touched the minds of farming and working youth throughout Japan who had been unable to acquire further education. He thus played a significant role in the movement to establish night schools for working youth that flourished after World War I.

Nitobe also became deeply involved in the problems of education for women. At that time there were essentially two streams of thought concerning the education of women. One emphasized obedience; the other, independence. In addition, there were already contrasting approaches in achieving a new education for women since the Meiji Restoration. For example, Fukuzawa Yukichi, the great liberalist of the early Meiji period, criticized the traditional Confucianist role of women in the social order. Fukuzawa took the position that in order to liberate women from the strict social mores placed upon them, it was necessary to re-educate men. Accordingly, in his writings on women, he stressed the importance of bringing about a change in the way men viewed women. Significantly, one of his major contributions to Japanese education was the founding of Keio University, a school for boys.

Another example is Naruse Jinzo. After studying education for girls in America, he founded Nihon Joshi Daigaku (Japan Women's University) as the first institution of higher learning for women in this country. Naruse promoted undergraduate education of women and advanced education for the teaching profession. In 1900, Tsuda Ume founded her famous college for girls, offering primarily English language and literature in a curriculum based on western culture. Such was the variety of approaches to women's education in Japan at that time.

Nitobe's ideas on the education of women were unique, contrasting with those of other leading figures of his day. He expressed deep interest in the emancipation of women through education from his earlier years onward. For example, writing in his diary while a student in his twenties at Johns Hopkins University, he expressed his desire to someday begin a girls' school in Japan. Nitobe's concern for women's education was influenced by his involvement with the Quaker movement in America. The fact that a Quaker woman of his acquaintance took an active interest in spreading Christianity in Japan through girls' education, which eventually came to fruition in the Friends' School for Girls, further deepened his interest in this endeavor.

Nitobe's faith led him to view all people as the creation of a God of love. Women, as human beings, should therefore receive an education that set them free from bondage. According to Nitobe, the traditional approach to the education of Japanese women, stressing the preparation of good wives and mothers obedient to their husbands, was misconceived. Rather, women should be considered human beings whose personalities deserve respect. To accomplish this, women should receive a form of useful education to enable them to achieve a degree of independence.

As president of a new university for women, Nitobe held the belief that there should be no distinction between education for men and that for women. In other words, women should receive an education similar to men's, since women have as much potential for growth as men. Women must receive some form of practical education, but not the type of vocational education provided for boys at that time. Rather, vocational education for either sex has a broad purpose and should be related to the development of personality and the search for truth. In addition to this emphasis, Nitobe believed that through Christianity the search for truth in learning—and science as well—should be pursued. An education founded on Christianity would develop the spiritual quality of the personality of the young student as well as her logical ability in science.

With this new vision for women's education, Nitobe accepted the challenge to become the first president of the Tokyo Women's Christian University (Tokyo Joshi Daigaku) in 1919. It was, he believed, a golden opportunity to apply his theories on the education of young women. Nitobe took an active interest in his students. He often visited classes, sitting with students and joining in the discussions. He then took lunch in the school dining room, eating with the students and exchanging ideas and opinions with them in an informal setting. Such was his abiding concern for the education of his students.

Because of an invitation to accept the position of Under Secretary of the League of Nations, Nitobe later had to resign as president to go to Switzerland. But under Nitobe's influence, the

Tokyo Women's Christian University became one of the most distinguished institutions for the higher education of women in modern Japan, with his students becoming active in various areas of society long after his death. As one example, Kawai Michiko, who later became a leader in the Young Women's Association of Japan, was the founder of Keisen Jogakuen, a girls' school.

His direct influence on the education of women in Japan extended far beyond that exerted in his work at Tokyo Women's Christian University. For example, he also became the principal of the Girls' School of Economics, currently the Tokyo Junior College of Culture (Tokyo Bunka Tankidai), where he applied more directly his ideas on vocational education for women. He also became directly and indirectly involved in a number of other institutions for women by serving as an advisor to such schools as Tsuda Women's College.

Because of his deep concern for the education of women, Nitobe wrote many articles on the subject for women's magazines in which he, a distinguished scholar, expressed his ideas in simplified form. He received many letters in response, especially from women experiencing various kinds of difficulties. Nitobe answered every letter and in the process became deeply sympathetic to the problems of women in Japanese society. He was constantly being consulted for advice, which he freely gave and which, as he described it, not only altered his ideas about women's education but changed his life as well. His attitude can be most clearly understood through his own words:

I have often seen old women worshipping stone statues of Jizo [a guardian deity of children] set up by the side of the road. Worshipping a stone statue of Jizo in itself is not a particularly profitable undertaking. Some people may rather think that it is nonsense. I feel differently. I respect such women's pious hearts. They piously worship such insignificant stone statues of Jizo. If such genuine devotion were directed toward something higher than Jizo, or if it were to go just one step further and accept the only living God, I wonder what sort of people would grow out of them. As I meditate along this line, my imagination on the possibility of these women's spiritual progress grows more and more.

In addition to his work in the field of women's education, one of Nitobe's most lasting contributions to Japanese education evolved through his role as principal of the First National Higher School (Daiichi Koto Gakko), the most exclusive institution preparing boys for Tokyo Imperial University. As an educational administrator with unique ideas, he began his career under difficult circumstances. Nationalistic thought was spreading throughout the cultural institutions of Japan at the beginning of this century, as evidenced by the school curriculum. *Shushin* (morals) had become the most prominent subject in the school curriculum based on the Imperial Rescript. By this time the nation was also bent on absorbing western technology as rapidly as possible. From 1903 on, the government tightly controlled textbook content and distribution in order to assure that the schools of Japan taught the precepts of an increasingly nationalistic government while at the same time fostering motivation to catch up with the West. The goal was none other than a modernized state with wealth and power.

In the midst of these developments, Nitobe was appointed principal of the First National Higher School in 1906. He immediately set about revising the traditional concepts of this state-run school that produced many, if not most, of the leaders of modern Japan. In order to better understand his role as principal of the most influential university preparatory school in the land, it is essential to consider Nitobe's basic ideas about higher education, which, in prewar Japan, included the upper secondary schools for boys aged seventeen to twenty.

The foundation of higher education, according to Nitobe, was liberal education—that is, the development of personality and character. It was of the greatest significance to him that each student come to an understanding of himself as an independent, self-conscious being in the process. In Nitobe's many books, articles, and lectures on morality, he urged students to ponder for themselves the great philosophical and spiritual questions of existence. He emphasized the relationship between "to be" and "to do," a topic which motivated considerable discussion among many of his students. "To be" concerned existence and the image of oneself. "To do" related to the practical application of one's life in service to the society and the nation. The two were interrelated and yet could be considered separately. The individual thus stands at the convergence of vertical and horizontal relations. Accordingly, one of the most important purposes of higher education to Nitobe was to develop one's personality in relation to a transcendental value, and to foster an attitude of responsibility to others from a social concern.

Having studied in both the United States and Europe, Nitobe concluded that Western universities and colleges originally aimed at bringing up good citizens. However, in the process of industrialization, the goals of American higher education underwent transformation; the aim became efficiency with a vocational emphasis. In Europe, Nitobe argued, things were different; for example, British higher education dominated by humanities stressed the development of a gentleman. In Germany the purpose of higher education was pure subjectivity: it was learning for learning's sake, representing the purest form of idealism.

Considering these various western approaches to higher education, Nitobe claimed that the true purpose of higher education was the liberation or emancipation of the individual. In Japanese national institutions of higher learning, the primary purpose was to prepare public servants. He accepted this purpose but argued that, in the process, the future leaders of Japan must experience a process of self-formation in the development of personality.

When Nitobe became the principal of the First National Higher School, the school was characterized by chauvinistic nationalism in the samurai tradition, a feudalistic concept carried over from the Tokugawa period into the modern era. Nitobe immediately set about transforming these characteristics with a new emphasis on humanitarian ideas. It was an attempt to liberalize the personalities of the future leaders of the nation by opening their spiritual eyes and broadening their perspectives. It was, in a sense, an effort to transform a school atmosphere that reflected a closed society into one that reflected an open society.

Nitobe was not opposed to nationalism in its broader meaning. He was indeed a patriot. A loyal citizen, he criticized contemporary Japanese education as one who loved his country deeply. For example, in *Weakness of Our Education*, published in 1906, he wrote:

No one can deny that our government has provided our schools with fine facilities. There is obviously a sharp difference between education during the Meiji period and that prior to the Meiji Restoration [1868]. There has been amazing growth and improvement in Japanese education during the Meiji period. Nevertheless, contemporary education deprives us of our humanity and is devoid of the spirit to love justice. We become mechanical in our total emphasis on acquiring knowledge. In the endless pursuit of scientific information for science's sake, and the quest for logical details, we become like machines. During my days as a student in an agricultural school, we studied modern agricultural technology as our most important subject. However, I could not help but think of things other than technology. The most important purpose in learning is not technology but an emancipated liberal spirit. The ultimate purpose of education is the emancipation of man.

Some students at the First National Higher School welcomed Nitobe's novel approach; others did not. Friction developed between the two groups. Yanaihara Tadao, later to become president of the University of Tokyo, recalls his days at the school only with fond memories, however:

When I was still a student in the First National Higher School, Dr. Nitobe was the principal, and he held open house for us students every Thursday from three until five or six in the afternoon. He rented a house for this purpose right next door to the school. At these gatherings he answered the various questions put to him by his students. He would serve tea and cookies, and we would have some very interesting conversations.

Dr. Yanaihara was one of many of Nitobe's students who assumed positions of great influence not only in prewar Japan but in the postwar period as well. Indeed, Nitobe's influence extended long after his death into the rebirth of democratic education during the preparation of the postwar Fundamental Law of Education, the foundation of democratic education in contemporary Japan. In the process of formulating the new law during the American Occupation, a special Council on Educational Reform (Kyoiku Sasshin Iinkai) was appointed to formulate the basic principles. Among this critical group were such people as Tanaka Kotaro, Morito Tatsuo, and Amano Teiyu, destined to become ministers of education, as well as Kawai Michiko, well-known female educator mentioned previously, and Nambara Shigeru, later president of the University of Tokyo. Each of these was deeply influenced by Nitobe as his former student who looked to his writings for guidance. And even after the Fundamental Law was promulgated in 1947, a number of those responsible for implementing the law—such as Ministers of Education Maeda Tamon and Abe Yoshishige, as well as the other ministers, Tanaka, Morito, and Amano, who served on the formulating committee—were all greatly influenced by Nitobe, having studied under him in the prewar era.

One of the most significant contributions Nitobe has made to contemporary Japanese education, then, has been through the work of his students who achieved critically important positions in postwar Japan. It was in no small measure through their efforts that the liberal trends in prewar Japan, characterized by Nitobe's thought, were released after the period of militaristic suppression. The postwar democratic reforms in education were certainly not all imported from America, but rather reflected to a very significant degree the prewar movements in Japan in which Nitobe played a major role.

The tolerance, flexibility, independence, and patience of earlier Japanese like Nitobe were essential to nurture democracy heralding a transformation in the spiritual values of Japan in the postwar era. Japan's postwar democracy is thus rooted in certain democratic ideas that were fostered in Japan long before World War II. We can, therefore, conclude that the thought and activities of Nitobe Inazo, a great Japanese educator, may exemplify the true and indigenous antecedents of the democratic thought of modern Japan.

The Life of Nitobe Inazo

1862   Born into a samurai family in Morioka.

1871   Adopted by his uncle after his father's death and moved to Edo (Tokyo).

1875   Entered Tokyo Eigo Gakko (later Preparatory School of Tokyo Imperial University).

1877   Entered Sapporo Agricultural College in September; baptized a Christian.

1881   Graduated from Sapporo Agricultural College; appointed an official of the Hokkaido Development Office.

1883   Entered Tokyo Imperial University to study English literature, economics, and statistics.

1884   Went to the United States and entered Allegheny College, Pennsylvania; in September, transferred to Johns Hopkins University.

1887   Appointed Assistant Professor at Sapporo Agricultural College; went to Germany for further study.

1890   Received the degree of Doctor of Philosophy from Halle University.

1891   Married Mary Patterson Elkinton, a Quaker, in Philadelphia; returned to Japan and was appointed professor at Sapporo Agricultural College.

1899   Received the degree of Doctor of Agriculture from the Ministry of Education; published *Bushido: The Soul of Japan*.

1901   Appointed to serve the Formosan government as head of the Industrial Development Bureau.

1903   Appointed Professor in the Law Department of Kyoto Imperial University.

1906   Received the degree of Doctor of Jurisprudence from Kyoto Imperial University; appointed Principal of the First National Higher School (Daiichi Koto Gakko).

1907   Published *Thoughts and Essays* and *Student-Days Abroad*.

1909   Appointed Associate Professor in the Law Department of Tokyo Imperial University.

1911	Sent to the U.S. as Japan's first exchange professor.
1913	Resigned the principalship of the First National Higher School; became a full professor in the Law Department, Tokyo Imperial University.
1915	Published *One Word A Day* and *Random Thoughts on Life*.
1916	Sent to the Philippines, Borneo, Celebes, Java, Singapore, Hong Kong, and Amoy.
1918	Appointed first President of Tokyo Women's Christian University.
1920	Appointed Under Secretary of the League of Nations.
1925	Chosen as a member of the Imperial Academy; received the degree of Doctor of Peers.
1929	Gave a speech of reproach in the House of Peers that caused the resignation of the Cabinet; elected director of the Institute of Pacific Relations.
1932	Received the honorary degree of LL.D. from Haverford College.
1933	Received the honorary degree of LL.D. from the University of Southern California; died in Victoria, Canada.

About the Author

Kiyoko Takeda Cho was born in 1917 in Hyogo Prefecture. She graduated from Kobe Jogakuin College in 1939, and from Olivet College in the United States in 1941. After studying at Columbia University and Union Theological Seminary, she returned to Japan and received her doctorate from the University of Tokyo in 1961. She joined the faculty of International Christian University in 1953, and retired as Graduate School Professor in 1988. She is the author of many publications in Japanese and, in English, of *The Dual Image of the Japanese Emperor* (1988).

Tsuda Ume in 1899.

Tsuda Ume

[1864-1929]

Takako Yamazaki

On August 6, 1900, Tsuda Ume wrote the following letter in English from Shiobara Hot Springs in Tochigi Prefecture to a friend, a Miss Kirk, in the United States:

I can imagine how busy you have been and all you have on your hands. I, too, have had such a spring and early summer! Now, however, I am taking a few weeks rest with Miss Bacon near the hot springs of Shiobara in the midst of the beautiful mountains. I cannot go into all the details of the backings and fillings in regard to my connection with the Peeresses' School (which was so hard to break). No one would believe me when I asked to resign and I had some fights to go through and some yet before me. But I am now *free* and have burned so to speak all my ships behind me. You have no idea what it is like to be connected with the Court and a Court School and to be regarded as a member (however humble) of the Imperial Household Department. However, I had to do it once and for all.

There were more reasons than merely the starting of the school that made me want to leave, but so you know I broke off a fifteen-year connection with the highest ranking school in Japan and gave up my official rank and title. All of this was worthless to me, but valued among our people. Most of my acquaintances were surprised, and many called to ask what was the matter, when it was published in the Official Gazette, but I am glad to say that I wanted to get away from all the conservatism and conventions of my life,

125

and now I am only a commoner, free to do what I like and free also from my salary, which however small, still in Japanese eyes was ample. You in democratic America cannot realize all this fuss, and I in my heart am glad to take my stand for what is right and true, and not for the rank and conventions and name.

And now, if I can only get my school building free from burdens, I am glad to go into the new work. Everyone tells me it is just the time to begin, and I have had so many encouraging words. My circulars are out, the school has been advertised, and I have had official permission to open.

I am now quite willing the thing should be open. There is no need for secrecy or for keeping it out of print now that my connection with the Court is severed, and I am only a private individual. No one knew of it out here, and all went well. Now there is no need of caution for me or for anyone, but perhaps it is too late to do much once the fever dies down. . . .

Miss Bacon is quite enthusiastic over the beginning, and we hope to do great things when once we begin. We are offering higher courses in English and preparation for the government examination for teacher's certificate in English, so we call it a School of English, but some day it will be more than that and will offer other courses of study.

Of the eighty or so letters from Tsuda Ume that are still extant, only this one deals in any detail with her thoughts and feelings concerning the opening of her private school. Differing from her other letters, this one expresses strong convictions that would seem to display her true inner state of mind about herself and her school. It was indeed the forerunner of the present Tsuda Women's College, approved by the Governor of Tokyo on July 26, 1900, that she was writing about with considerable excitement.

At the time of this letter, there was little sympathy in Japan with the education of women. In fact there was only one institution where a woman could gain the benefits of higher education: the national Higher Normal School for Girls in Tokyo (known today as Ochanomizu Women's University), which did not in-

The five young girls chosen to study in the United States, prior to their departure in 1871. Tsuda is second from the right.

Tsuda as a student at Bryn Mawr College, Philadelphia, ca. 1890.

Photograph commemorating the opening of Tsuda Ume's Girls' School of English, 1900. Tsuda, at far left, stands next to Alice Bacon.

Tsuda in her later years.

clude a Department of English Literature. Tsuda Ume was on its faculty while simultaneously teaching at the Peeresses' School. Her annual income was 800 yen, a fairly substantial sum. Her position also had considerable status in the eyes of the Japanese. Had she continued to lead this lifestyle, she could well have lived comfortably for the rest of her life.

The Dean of the Peeresses' School was Shimoda Utako, a leading figure in girls' education during the Meiji period. However, Tsuda and Shimoda held almost diametrically opposite opinions concerning education. Since it was not Tsuda's nature to criticize others, we must look elsewhere to learn why she decided to make her own independent way through life.

According to the letter, the reason for Tsuda's resignation from the Peeresses' School was not only that she wanted to start her own school but also that she wanted to live a life of righteousness and truth. In other words, she resigned so she could attempt to fulfill her desire to live as a human being in search of a justification for living. That explains her fervent wish to break loose from the conventions that constrained her and to make her way freely through life as she saw fit.

For Tsuda Ume, education was not the learning of ordinary customs, habits, and manners but the nurturing of the ability to distinguish between worth and worthlessness, and knowing the merits of truth so that a sense of ultimate justification could be developed. These concepts ultimately led her to found her school, which eventually developed into the distinguished Tsuda Women's College.

There is an earlier letter to the same Miss Kirk dated August 31, 1894. The Sino-Japanese War had been declared on the first of August, and the letter touches on this:

This year has been a very hard one, and now the war news is becoming more and more serious. They say that we are in for a three years war, and all our best men are being sent over, and so much money is being collected. Poor Japan is making desperate efforts, but at the very best, war is such a terrible thing. It makes one realize it, to be on the spot, and I think that it is such a savage and horrible thing. To think of men, deliberately setting out to murder one another—for that is virtually what it is. We have had an anxious summer in Tokyo.

Tsuda's penetrating insights had a keenness sharpened by her sense of freedom. Her thoughts are simply those of a free human being, often original and fresh. There were good reasons for that. In her later years she described her life in the descriptive term of a "unique destiny" because it was so unusual. Few would disagree.

Born on December 31, 1864, in the Ushigome district of Edo, Tsuda Ume was the second daughter of Tsuda Sen and his wife Hatsuko. Although they were most intimately concerned with her future, there was also an American couple, the Charles Lanmans, who had a profound influence on her, for they were in effect her second parents. The intermediary between the Lanmans and Ume's natural parents was the Development Agency, established during the first year of the Meiji era for the promotion of the northern island of Hokkaido.

The greatest immediate factor bearing on Ume's future was the progressive thinking of her samurai father, whose master, Hotta Masayoshi, was so enthusiastic about the introduction of western culture into Japan that he was given the nickname Ranpeki, literally "Dutch-affected." At the time of the uproar caused by the arrival of Commodore Matthew Perry's Black Ships, Ume's father was a seventeen-year-old youth serving in the defense of Edo, the capital. He came into direct contact with some of the foreign visitors in connection with his duties, encounters that led him to the realization that the study of western civilization was essential. Soon after, he sought out a teacher, changed his subject of interest from Dutch to English, and began studying assiduously. Tsuda was appointed by the Shogunate as an interpreter in the Foreign Affairs Bureau of the government in April 1862, at a time when the exclusion policy had become highly controversial. In fact, the personal safety of a scholar of western studies was not assured. It was exactly two years later that his wife gave birth to Ume.

Tsuda Sen became so obsessed with western culture that in 1867, while spending half a year in America on Shogunate business, he sent the following note to his wife: "I can see no point in maintaining a topknot in this country. I decided to cut it off because it's embarassing." His shorn topknot, symbolic of the samurai [warrior] class, was included with the note. This caused much consternation and distress to his family, for the governmental order to remove topknots and swords was not issued until four years later.

Tsuda Sen was deeply impressed by two aspects of life in America. First, there appeared to be no class distinctions. To him, equality existed among all the people. Second, American agriculture was based on scientific principles. Consequently, immediately after the Meiji Restoration in 1868, he left government service for private enterprise, establishing the Gakunosha, an agriculture school, and publishing the *Agriculture Magazine*. As a Meiji liberal and an agriculturalist, he devoted the rest of his life to agricultural reformation in Japan. He personally pioneered several new concepts in agriculture in Japan by initiating such schemes as the planting of roadside trees, the cultivation of vegetables foreign to Japan, and the management of a large-scale farm.

A letter sent by Uchimura Kanzo, the famous Christian scholar of the period, marking the eight hundredth edition of *Agriculture Magazine* in July 1902, shows Tsuda Sen's originality and ingenuity:

> Your modern methods of farming, which have been practiced in our country for over thirty years, have had a history equal to the length of that of the Meiji government. But what is more important is that they have made a contribution to the lives of all people in the nation. . . . Your approach to agriculture is, first, the method of farming for a modern society. Second, it is the agriculture of the common farmer, not of government officials and administrators, who can only take pride in decorations of high rank. And third, it is an agriculture that develops self-reliance according to the principles of feudalism.

In a similar fashion, Nitobe Inazo praised Tsuda Sen in a eulogy written for the *Kokumin Shimbun* on April 27, 1907:

> It was his ideas that made one admire the man as well as

his beliefs. As you may well know, at that time anyone with even a minor rank could carve out a career for himself in the area of law or politics. Tsuda was a well-respected official of the Shogunate administration, so had he wished to advance himself he would have become quite a prominent person. But without second thoughts he stepped down from being a government official to become a common man, a farmer. It is remarkable that he invested all his efforts and assets in the scientific cultivation of fruit trees and vegetables, as well as in the creation of pastureland for cattle. In doing so, he taught the whole nation that agriculture is not just planting and harvesting, and founded the scientific approach to agriculture of today.

In 1875 Sen and Hatsuko were baptized into the Christian faith and became the first Japanese to become members of the Methodist Church in Tokyo. But no matter how open Sen was to western culture, it is unlikely that he would have sent his seven-year-old daughter Ume to the United States without the call from the Hokkaido Development Agency for girls to study abroad. That eventful moment took place in the autumn of 1871.

The plan to send young Japanese girls abroad to study had been devised by the Assistant Secretary of the Agency, Kuroda Kiyotaka. In January 1871 he had set out on an inspection tour of European and American developmental enterprises. He first visited the United States, where he invited General Horace Caplon to become a consultant to the Agency. Then, together with the General, he proceeded to Europe before passing through America once again on his return journey to Japan. During his two visits to the U.S. he was impressed by the apparent equality between the sexes and the fact that elementary education was provided for the masses. He had many discussions with Mori Arinori, the Japanese High Commissioner to Washington, over conditions in America and his beliefs that the status of women in Japan was very low in comparison with that in western countries. Kuroda believed that no matter how his agency planned the development of Hokkaido, it would not be very successful if only poorly educated people were sent there. It was essential to send well-educated, trained people. Women were the most intimately concerned with education, particularly in the early years of child development in Japan. Accordingly, in Kuroda's view, girls' education should be given first priority in order to render the Hokkaido Development Enterprise a success. The government had already sent boys to study in Britain and America. Now it was time to seriously consider sending girls abroad.

Kuroda returned to Japan in July 1871 convinced of his beliefs. He submitted a position paper on the promotion of education, including that for selected girls' education abroad, to the government, explaining that the Development Agency could bear the cost of such a program. The timing was just right for his proposal. In August, Emperor Meiji abolished clans, established a prefectural system of local government, and recognized meritorious service that, among other things, recommended foreign travel for the nobility. It also included statements about the necessity of formal education for women as well as the advisability of foreign travel for women of the nobility class. In this atmosphere of social reform, Kuroda's recommendation was immediately adopted by the government, and permission was given to the Development Agency to begin accepting applications from girls who wanted to study abroad.

It is quite possible that if the reforming zeal of the early Meiji era had continued with the same intensity toward the absolute emancipation of women, the subsequent history of Japan might have been completely different. Still, it was as if a window had suddenly been opened and rays of light poured into a long-darkened room. One of those on whom the light fell was Tsuda Ume, for her father promptly submitted an application for her to study abroad. Considering that she was barely seven years old, her father's uncommon resolve and foresight were remarkable. Indeed, in later years she was to reflect upon her "unique destiny."

Five girls were initially recruited by the Development Agency and sent to the United States. In December of 1871, they set sail from Yokohama on the same ship carrying the famous Iwakura Mission on its grand inspection tour of North America and Europe. Unfortunately, two of the girls became ill shortly after arriving in America and had to be sent home, but the other three, who remained in the United States for over a decade, became lifelong friends. They were Tsuda Ume, Yamakawa Sutematsu, and Nagai Shigeko. The latter two were to provide invaluable assistance to Ume in her later undertaking of the Tsuda Girls' School of English.

Ume was put under the care of Charles Lanman, who, together with his wife, raised her in their home in the Washington suburbs of Georgetown for the next eleven years. Yamakawa Sutematsu was entrusted to Dr. Leonard Bacon, whose youngest daughter, Alice, provided the direct motivation for the fulfillment of Ume's aim in life of establishing a private college for women. Alice Bacon later came to Japan to offer her assistance. It was this woman, vacationing with Ume, who was referred to in the letter that opens this essay.

The period from Ume's arrival in the United States until her return to Japan at the age of eighteen corresponded to the present period of formal education in elementary, junior high, and senior high schools. There are individual differences, of course, but it is during these years that most of a person's formative features are developed. Although it was her progressive father who sent her to America, it was the Lanmans who warmly welcomed her into their home and who played the leading role in raising her to womanhood.

Charles Lanman was the Secretary of the Japanese High Commission in Washington at the time. From his own account, his father was a frontiersman and his mother a woman of mixed French and American Indian descent. It was probably from this background that he acquired a love for nature in his boyhood and a fondness for roaming through the forests of America. In contrast, he was also extremely fond of reading and writing. He wrote and published over thirty works, which were considered to have the highest literary merit. In addition, he was interested in art and decorated his house with works of fine art, antiques, and paintings, including some of his own creation.

Charles Lanman's wife, Adeline, was the daughter of a successful businessman who had moved to Georgetown from New England. Upon the wedding of his daughter, he presented her with a traditional duplex house as a gift. This was the house that welcomed Ume. It is clear from Adeline's letters to Ume's mother in Japan that she was a deeply affectionate woman of warm sensitivity. She and her husband raised Ume lovingly, as if she were their own daughter. They had no children of their own. The home in which Ume was placed, then, typified the cultural intelligentsia of the eastern United States in the early 1870s.

Under the careful guidance of the Lanmans, who possessed both a pioneering spirit and a progressive attitude, Ume was able to settle down very quickly and go on to complete elementary school and junior high school in the United States. She completed school at the Stephenson Seminary and then received her high-school education at the Archer Institute. Both schools were small private institutions of about one hundred students. With so few students it was possible for each to receive a thorough education on an individual basis. This made a lasting impression on Ume. She made good use of her own personal experiences and employed similar methods when she opened her English school for girls in Japan later on.

The first ten-year period of study abroad was terminated in 1881 when a notification arrived from the Development Agency informing her to prepare to return to Japan. Nagai Shigeko, who had some problems with her health, returned to Japan that year, but Tsuda Ume and Yamakawa Sutematsu requested a one-year postponement of their return so that they could graduate from their respective schools. This was granted by the Agency, and the girls returned to Japan late the following year, but not before the Agency, which had sent them abroad to study, was disbanded. The two girls went back to Japan in November, some nine months after the Agency was officially abolished. This brought an end to the imaginative scheme typical of the bold, almost unrestrained, initiatives in the field of education for women promoted by the educational policies of the early Meiji period. The fire of reform had gradually burnt itself out, since no subsequent group of girls was sent abroad for study. Rather, education for women, instead of being promoted by the government, came to be increasingly developed by foreign missionaries, as can be seen from the following list of schools for girls established during early Meiji:

Missionary Schools

1870   Ferris School for Girls in Yokohama

1871   United School for Girls (Kyoritsu)
        in Yokohama
1874   Aoyama Institute for Girls in Tokyo
1875   Kobe Institute for Girls in Kobe
        Heian Institute for Girls in Kyoto
1876   Tokyo Academy for Girls
1877   Rikkyo Institute for Girls (St. Paul's
        College) in Tokyo
1878   Doshisha School for Girls in Kyoto
1879   Kassui School for Girls in Nagasaki

                 Government School
1872   Tokyo Jogakko (Girls' School)

After Tsuda's return to Japan, she was confronted with the immediate problem of finding suitable employment. The Development Agency had been abolished and the emancipation of women had progressed little during the eleven years she had been abroad. She had received a formal education in America, but in Japan she found herself in the predicament of no longer having a use to which to put her education. However, in spite of the anguish of searching for a new career, the crisis did serve to provide her with another opportunity to study abroad.

On November 3, 1883, at a ball held at the Rokumeikan, she met Ito Hirobumi, the great statesman, for the second time. They had first met in 1871 when Ume sailed to America in the company of the Iwakura Mission, of which Ito was a member. He was now a very influential person in the Japanese political world. He first asked Tsuda to become a private tutor to the Ito family. Later he introduced her to the principal of a private school for girls, where she would not only teach English but also study Japanese. Then, in 1885, upon the recommendation of Ito, she was appointed to teach at the newly founded Peeresses' School, where she taught for fifteen years.

Tsuda's feelings about this period were frankly expressed in the letter that she wrote to Miss Kirk from Shiobara Hot Springs. In the eyes of most people she had attained the highest possible status in society, a position of distinction and honor. Yet she herself was not much impressed with her accomplishments. It might have been different had she experienced the joy of teaching serious students, but it was not possible to give a rigorous education to the girls of the Peeresses' School, who had been brought up in high society. Even though they were well-mannered and gentle, very few of them had any strong, well-defined personality traits.

Shortly after being appointed to the teaching staff of the Peeresses' School, Tsuda was consulted about bringing a foreigner to Japan to teach at the school. She unhesitatingly recommended her friend Alice Bacon for the position. Alice Bacon was then teaching at a school in Hampton, Virginia. Nevertheless she immediately responded to the invitation and came to Japan for one year to take up the position of lecturer at the Peeresses' School.

Alice Bacon was six years older than Tsuda. She had already decided on her own career, evidenced by her teaching position at a special school for underprivileged black and American Indian children. When she learned about Tsuda's troubles she immediately urged her to go abroad again to study. She specifically recommended that her friend go to the United States for higher education. Thanks to her having tenure at the Peeresses' School, the road to further study was quickly opened to Tsuda by the government. In July 1889 she was able to set out from Yokohama, leaving Alice Bacon in Japan to finish her term of appointment.

Half a year earlier, on February 11, the Meiji Constitution had been promulgated. The following year, on October 30, the Imperial Rescript on Education was issued. In the nearly twenty-year interval between her first departure from Yokohama during the Meiji period in 1871 and her second departure in 1889, Japan had changed immensely. Therefore, Tsuda's problems were not just her own but those of all Japanese women. She was setting out in search of a new way and a fresh purpose in life for Japanese women as a whole.

Tsuda's destination was Bryn Mawr College in Philadelphia, which had been founded as a women's college. In 1885, Dr. Joseph W. Taylor, a devout believer in the Quaker faith, established the college based on an educational policy in accordance with Quaker beliefs, setting a school tradition of strictness, modesty, and trustworthiness. Bryn Mawr College was a fairly small institution of about 150 students at the time of Tsuda's residence. She had not decided what she would study when she left Yokohama, but upon enrollment she elected to specialize in biology, registering as a non-regular student for a two-year period.

Tsuda had always shown an inclination for literature, but she quickly revealed an aptitude for science as well. It was most appropriate that she should wish to study and do research in the new, wide-open field of science in an attempt to discover the essence of life. In doing so, she was without doubt following in her agriculturalist father's footsteps. Her research in biology reached a peak with her dissertation, "The Orientation of the Frog's Egg," which was the culmination of joint research conducted with Professor Thomas Hunt Morgan from 1891 to the winter of 1892, during her second year of study. This dissertation was published in *The Quarterly Journal of Microscopical Science* in 1894, becoming the first paper published by a Japanese woman in the field of natural science. However, even though she had attained such academic achievements, her "unique destiny" once more intervened to prevent her from following the normal path of a scientist devoted to a life of biological research.

Alice Bacon returned to America in the summer of 1890. This ultimately proved to be an important event in Tsuda's life, for upon her return Bacon began writing a book entitled *Japanese Girls and Women*, based upon the notes that she had taken during her one-year stay in Japan. These were essentially observations and commentaries on her personal experiences and the customs and traditions she had witnessed on various trips throughout Japan during her appointment at the Peeresses' School. However, Bacon was soon faced with many unforeseen problems and questions in her writing, so that she could hardly wait until Tsuda's summer vacation began in order to invite her to the Hampton home to seek her assistance. The two of them spent every day talking together from dawn till dusk, discussing the situation faced by Japanese women.

By the end of the summer Tsuda was convinced that her life's work lay in the development of higher education for Japanese women, because she believed it would be impossible to develop

Japanese culture without establishing educational opportunities for women at the same level as those for men. She was well aware that education for men had made tremendous gains since the Meiji Reformation, whereas education for women had made little progress. Except for the Normal School for Girls in Tokyo, there were no institutions of higher education for women established by the government. Tsuda came to feel that her mission in life was to open a college for women.

Tsuda revealed her plans to Miss Bacon and asked her to come to Japan to help when the time was right. Alice Bacon was only too glad to be asked and readily promised her support. As can be seen in the previously quoted letter sent from Shiobara Hot Springs some ten years later, they were not building castles in the air. The excitement generated by their discussions in Hampton was not forgotten in Shiobara after permission had been granted to open a private school. They were now experiencing anticipation and trepidation at turning their dreams into reality and making a fresh start in life.

Tsuda's scheduled period of study in the United States had been two years, but this was extended to three years so that she could devote the summer of the extra year to work related to the education of Japanese women. Her efforts were concentrated on the raising of contributions toward a fund with a projected endowment of $8,000, called the American Scholarship for Japanese Women. This was a plan designed to send one student to study in the United States every four years by means of the interest earned on the principal. From her own experiences Tsuda wished that her fellow countrywomen could experience the same good fortune in America that she had.

In 1892, upon the completion of her course of studies at Bryn Mawr College, she was asked to remain in the United States to continue her research. It was a tempting offer that would probably not be made again, but Tsuda resolved that she would return to Japan. The decision to devote herself to the interests of Japanese women, made during the summer at Hampton, was confirmed in her rejection of this attractive offer. She would have been the first of the Japanese intelligentsia to remain in America for advanced academic studies had she accepted the university's invitation. However, she showed herself to be true to the traditions of her samurai ancestors.

On September 14, 1900, a simple ceremony was held in a ten-mat room of a rented house at 15 Kojimachi, in the heart of Tokyo, to mark the opening of Tsuda Ume's Girls' School of English. Seventeen people were present: teachers, ten students, and guests, among whom was Tsuda's friend Duchess Oyama. The ceremony consisted of a recitation of the Imperial Rescript on Education, hymns, prayers, a reading from the Bible in English, and a statement of Tsuda Ume's goals outlining the new school's objectives. Speaking in Japanese from a prepared manuscript written in English, she gave the gist of what constituted education in her view:

> Education is something which can be received without modern buildings or facilities. I believe that a genuine education is something far surpassing the worth of material furnishings. It is achieved by competent teachers and the will and desire of students to study. . . . In large-scale schools where many students have to be taught together at one time, it is not possible to obtain satisfactory results. All that can be done is the imparting of facts and information. Genuine education cannot be carried out teaching such large numbers of students in big classrooms. It is essential to deal with each student separately in accordance with [her] individual character because I believe that people's hearts and minds are as different as their faces. Therefore, in order to make genuine education a reality, it is necessary to limit the number of students in the classroom. . . . The English Institute has various objectives and not the least of these is the provision of authoritative instruction and guidance for those women who wish to obtain a license as an instructor of the English language. At the moment, our school is so insignificant that it barely casts a shadow, but in the future, as a place which gives women the opportunity of work worthy of their abilities, it will be an absolutely indispensable institution. . . .
>
> I would like to draw attention to one or two matters which I think deserve a certain amount of caution. When

following a [specialized] course of learning there is an almost inevitable tendency for a person's way of thinking to
become narrowed. While making efforts to apply yourself
to the [specialized] study of English it will not do for you
to neglect those matters indispensable to a mature woman. . . .

   This institution is the first school ever to provide a higher
[specialized] education for young women. I am aware that
because of this it will readily attract the attention of the
public and be criticized in various ways. The methods of
tuition and the nature of the courses which are offered will
not be criticized as much as insignificant matters such as
the lack of refined language in everyday speech, bad manners when meeting people not connected to the school, and
neglect of the accepted rules of etiquette and dress. This
criticism of such triviality will then be used to determine
the merit of the whole enterprise. I would like to ask you,
then, to not be overly conspicuous or too obtrusive, but
always to exhibit grace and modesty, civility and care in
anything and everything. Such manners need not by any
means clash with the ultimate objective of further study.

Tsuda's first two comments constituted her idea of education
and the desirability of small classes. These make up the nucleus
of her philosophy. She followed this with a statement on the
necessity of providing vocational training and guidance but
warned of the danger of overspecialization and the consequent
neglect of education of the whole person. Looking at the four
main points of her speech, it is evident that (1) material resources
are not absolutely essential for a good education, (2) education
must be adapted to the differing personalities of the students,
(3) education should avoid overspecialization and attempt to
cultivate the whole person, and (4) education is to provide sufficient training in specialized skills that will enable women to
achieve economic independence. These points are noteworthy
as a statement of an educational philosophy that, considering
the period, may be said to be a declaration of independence
by a surprisingly progressive woman.
   As Tsuda was about to make such an education a reality, she

reminded her students to heed some prudent advice. The Girls' School of English was the first private institution to offer higher education for women. Above all, it was important to take particular care lest over some triviality the school receive unpleasant criticism that could impede the very aim of the entire enterprise—namely, higher education for women. The social norms of that time and the experience of Tsuda herself, who had constantly suffered from trifling criticisms aimed at mistakes that she had unwittingly committed, were no doubt at the back of her mind. It should be noted, though, that she was well aware of how revolutionary her venture was for Japanese women.

The only profession available for women at the time was teaching. Tsuda had herself been a member of the Ministry of Education's Committee for the Certification of Teachers of the English Language, but had resigned from this post before the founding of her institute, an act indicative of her sense of propriety. She had a distaste for fame, precedent, trend, and fashion. The latter dislike became evident some years later, around 1911, when phrases such as *new women* and *modern women* became popular. Tsuda was not in the least taken in by them; nor were the majority of her students. It would seem that she was more interested in searching for the causes of change rather than riding with the tides of popular movements that promised much but were all too often washed away in the sands of time.

The name of the initial ceremony is shown in the school's official records as the "ceremony for the opening of classes." This took place on a Friday, yet classes did not actually begin until the following Monday because Saturday was designated a holiday and Sunday was reserved for attending church services. It is surprising that a school embodying such substantial connotations of social change had begun in such a modest form.

Two years later, in April 1902, Alice Bacon, who had so faithfully kept her promise of more than ten years, returned to the United States. She had worked devotedly as Tsuda's personal assistant, helping to ensure that the foundations of the school were in place. In the following month, Anna Cope Hartshorne arrived as her replacement. The two had first met at Bryn Mawr College during Tsuda's second period of study abroad. However, even before this they had been bound by a unique twist of fate.

When Tsuda Sen visited the United States in 1867, one of the books he brought back with him was a treatise of western medical practice entitled *The Essentials of the Principles and Practice of Medicine*. The author of this work was Dr. Henry Hartshorne, Anna's father. The book was translated into Japanese and published in 1872. At that time Japanese medicine consisted of either the traditional Chinese methods or the methods learned at the Dutch schools. The book was held in high esteem and sold so well that Henry Hartshorne took the opportunity to visit Japan. He visited a second time in 1895 at the age of 70, and resolved to settle down in Japan and to be buried there. Dr. Hartshorne was a devout Quaker who gave the rest of his life in the service of love. He died at his home in the Tsukiji district of Tokyo in 1897.

With the foundation of her school, there was no valid reason to prevent Tsuda from requesting aid and support from persons in high society or in official circles. Because of her status, she would have been quite suited to doing so. However, with her final resignation from public office, she announced that she was turning her back on those sectors of society she considered so heavily tainted with fabrication and falsehood. She requested assistance only from those people in whom she had complete faith and to whom she could reveal her private resolve. Fortunately, she was endowed with true friends who sincerely wished to help her. Alice Bacon and Anna Hartshorne devoted all their energy to the development of higher education for Japanese women, yet worked without remuneration from the school.

Tsuda Ume had been baptized into the Christian faith on the evening of July 13, 1873, while she was still in the care of the Lanmans. From the letters that Mrs. Lanman wrote to the girl's mother, it seems that they had not especially encouraged Ume to adopt their faith. Rather, she had naturally done so as a result of the atmosphere of the Lanman household as well as through regular Sunday School attendance. When they learned of Ume's wish to be baptized, the Lanmans chose to have her join a specific religious body, the independent Old Swedes Church in Bridgeport, northwestern Philadelphia, where a friend, the Reverend Octavius Perinchief, was pastor. The Lanmans themselves were members of the Episcopal Church. Initially their intention was only to have Ume christened, but her responses were so positive that, at nine years of age, she became the first Japanese woman to receive baptism into the Christian faith abroad. Ume's own parents were to be baptized in January 1875. Thus, in the space of one and a half years, the whole Tsuda family became Christians.

After the opening of the school, Tsuda was very strict about the dormitory students' observance of the Sabbath, although she never actively promoted Christianity herself. She was fully aware that religious belief was a personal issue not to be overtly emphasized, no matter how significant she believed it to be. For her, Christianity was the foundation of education. Although it was not officially in the rules and regulations of the school, the reading of the Bible during the opening ceremony was sufficient to indicate that the school was fundamentally a Christian college. However, it was not a mission school, as Tsuda entertained serious doubts about the worth of such institutions. She did not believe in the policy of requiring students to adopt Christianity through coercion. Furthermore, she was apprehensive about education given solely by foreign teachers, who would almost inevitably neglect aspects of Japan that should be taught to the students.

Tsuda herself had spent such a long time abroad during her early life that she had forgotten much of the Japanese language. Nevertheless, she had a strong love for her native land. Her feelings are evident in a letter written in English as a response to a request from Mr. Lanman. Dated May 31, 1875, the letter was composed some two years after her baptism, when she was still a young girl of eleven. She stated that Japan had no need to imitate foreign countries but should maintain its own traditions except for one aspect: It would be better if all Japanese became Christians and all idols—Buddhist statues and figures—were destroyed. To alleviate the cost of constructing churches, she naively wrote, "change a few things in the temples and they will make beautiful churches." It can be seen that she was a very devout Christian even then. In later years Tsuda did not speak so candidly on matters of faith, but there is no doubt that her views on education and humankind embodied the freedom of religious faith.

In May 1917, after seventeen years of strenuous work, Tsuda became ill with diabetes. Excerpts from her diary reveal her frustration and grief at collapsing at the "height of her career." The illness was irreversible, however, and in a short time controlled her life completely. She had to eat in accordance with her doctor's instructions and ensure that the quantity of food she consumed was carefully weighed. Even her illness could be viewed as divine providence, however, for she was able once more to employ her knowledge of natural science that had become half forgotten since her graduation from Bryn Mawr College.

Tsuda fulfilled a life of faith in God as a member of the Episcopal Church, the denomination to which the Lanmans had introduced her. According to people who knew her in later years, she kept by her bedside strips of paper on which she wrote the names of people for whom she felt obliged to pray. They recollect that she unfailingly committed those names to memory before she offered prayers for them. For Tsuda, who had led such an active life since childhood, the twelve years of reading and prayer that she spent in this later part of her life was probably a form of peace on earth.

Her diary entry for August 16, 1929, consists of only one line, and that one in English: "Storm last night." This storm was part of a typhoon that had approached Japan from the south of the island of Shikoku, came ashore at the Kitan Straits, and passed through Osaka before blowing itself out in the Japan Sea. After she had recorded in her diary the tempest of the previous night, she quietly passed away at nine o'clock in the evening of the sixteenth at her cottage in the seaside town of Kamakura. She was sixty-five years old.

Tsuda Ume's life, beginning with her studies in America as a child, had been one of giving unsparingly of everything she valued. She devoted herself to the task of establishing her school with such effort that eventually she collapsed from an illness that gradually sapped her strength and led to her death. Perhaps she listened to the storm while reflecting on her path through life.

Tsuda is thought to have written one sonnet, which she composed at the Oswego State School while studying education and teaching methods there for half a year during her second period of study abroad. It is supposed to have been composed at the beginning of 1891, and reveals the writer's faith as she thrust herself forward on her way through life after the decisive summer at Hampton the year before:

The Ocean Voyage

The ocean wide and bleak before me lay;
Naught o'er and round me but the dusky sky
And waters deep and dark; the loud shrill cry
Of seagulls into silence died away;
With fear I saw the fading light of day,
And thro' the darkness dim of eve watched I
How wind and waves did roughly vie
Our ship to toss, as if with toy they played;
Yet knew I well that o'er those stormy seas,
The skillful pilot guides the vessel frail,
'Ere long to reach the distant promised land.
So in the fitful changes of the breeze
As her life's stormy main we darkly sail,
With faith we trust our Father's guiding hand.

The Life of Tsuda Ume

1864   Born in Edo (Tokyo), the second daughter of Tsuda Sen.

1871   Sent to America at age seven for study by the Hokkaido Development Office. Departed in a group of five girls from Yokohama in December, together with the members of the Iwakura Mission.

1872   Arrived in Washington, D.C., to take up residence with the Charles Lanman family in Georgetown. Entered Stephenson Seminary.

1873   Baptized at Old Swedes Church of Bridgeport in Philadelphia.

1878   Graduated from Stephenson Seminary and entered Archer Institute.
1882   Graduated from Archer Institute and returned to Japan.
1883   Taught English at Tsukiji Kaigan Women's School.
1886   Joined the faculty of the Peeresses' School in Tokyo.
1889   Departed from Yokohama for study in the U.S. Entered Bryn Mawr College and specialized in biology.
1892   Completed the course at Bryn Mawr College and returned to Japan to continue teaching at the Peeresses' School.
1898   Joined the faculty of the Higher Normal School for Girls in Tokyo while continuing to teach at the Peeresses' School.
1900   Resigned teaching positions. Opened the Girls' School of English (forerunner of Tsuda Women's College) and became chief administrator.
1901   Started publication of the *Eigakushinpō* (English Literature Gazette).
1915   Received the Order of the Sacred Crown from the Emperor.
1917   Became ill with diabetes.
1919   Retired as active administrator of her school.
1929   Died on August 16 at her villa in Kamakura.

About the Author

Takako Yamazaki was born in 1920 in Hyogo Prefecture. She graduated from Tsuda School of English in 1942, and from Kyushu Imperial University in 1945. She joined the faculty of Tsuda College in 1945, and is now Emeritus Professor there. Her publications (in Japanese) include *Umeko Tsuda* (1962) and *The Writings of Umeko Tsuda*.

Sawayanagi Masataro in 1925.

Sawayanagi Masataro

[1865-1927]

Hiroshi Mizuuchi

Sawayanagi Masataro was a distinguished educator who played
a leading role in developing educational theory for more than
thirty years, from the late nineteenth century to the first quarter
of this century. This was an era of rapid industrial development
and drastic social and cultural changes, including a sharp expansion of the school system; internationally also it was a time
of enormous consequence, encompassing the First World War.
Sawayanagi was one of the most prominent figures who provided
direction for Japanese education during this historical period
of political and social upheaval.

The scope of Sawayanagi's activities was extremely broad.
Few Japanese educators have equaled the illustrious career of
this colorful figure. After graduating from the Department of
Philosophy of the Tokyo Imperial University in 1888, Sawayanagi initially held a position in school administration at the
Ministry of Education. However, he resigned from that office
in 1892, and subsequently held posts as principal at both public
and private secondary schools for a number of years.

Sawayanagi then returned to the Ministry of Education as
director of a bureau and was subsequently promoted to the post
of Vice Minister of Education, the top professional position in
the Ministry. As a high government official, Sawayanagi devoted
himself to the improvement of education in modern Japan. He
demonstrated his ability by establishing senior high schools,
higher normal schools, and universities and by bringing about
a two-year extension of compulsory education. Illness forced
him to resign once again from the Ministry, however. Upon his

149

recovery he became the first president of Tohoku Imperial University, followed by the prestigious presidency of Kyoto Imperial University. It was during his term as president of Tohoku Imperial University that he took the decisive step of admitting women to the university before their acceptance at other Imperial universities attracted much attention throughout the nation.

Sawayanagi also attempted to initiate university reforms during his term of office at Kyoto Imperial University. However, a conflict with the faculty over his policies compelled him to resign prematurely when he attempted to fire seven professors who had no notable academic achievements. The law department opposed this action as a violation of academic freedom, and the controversy became known in Japanese educational history as the Sawayanagi Incident at Kyoto University.

Sawayanagi's distinguished reputation is thus attributed to his contributions to Japanese education as a leading official of the Ministry of Education, as a secondary-school principal, and as a university president, in addition to his energetic activities as a leader of the so-called Taisho New Movement in Education, which evolved during the dozen or so years of the Taisho era (1912–26). Sawayanagi was one of the most influential leaders in developing theory and practice within this movement.

The involvement in the New Movement began in April 1917, when Sawayanagi established the Seijo Elementary School as an experimental institution based on the emerging progressive principles of education. Up until then, the New Movement had been developed mainly at elementary schools affiliated with normal or higher normal schools. In contrast with the experiments under way in these schools, Sawayanagi's Seijo Elementary School was one of the few private schools taking the initiative in the theoretical and practical reform of education. Other schools—such as Jiyu Gakuen, founded by Hani Motoko; Teikoku Elementary School, launched by Nishiyama Tetsuji; Seikei Elementary School, established by Nakamura Shunji; and Jido no Mura (Children's Village) Elementary School, started by Noguchi Entaro and Nomura Yoshihei—participated in this progressive movement in education. Sawayanagi, however, played perhaps the leading role in promoting the New Move-

Sawayanagi (seated at left) in 1885, while a student.

In his study, 1926, shortly before his death.

ment in Education while serving as president of Teikoku Kyōiku-kai (the Imperial Society for Education), a massive nationwide organization of teachers.

In his later years Sawayanagi looked back upon his life and wrote: "I was a wanderer in the field of education." He had, in fact, provoked a great sensation in the educational world in those days: a famous educator who served as president of one of the most prominent Imperial universities as well as principal of a junior and senior high school, he had subsequently resigned the powerful position as Vice Minister of Education to become the principal of a small private elementary school. He had concluded from his experiences at the various levels of education that the development of primary education for the common people would determine the destiny of the Japanese race and the nation itself. For this reason Sawayanagi put his heart and soul into the study and reform of primary education in Japan.

Reflecting his wide interests, Sawayanagi also became a prolific writer. He wrote over fifty books, including translated works, and over two hundred articles, such as "*Teikoku Kyoiku*" (Imperial Education) and "*Kyoiku Mondai Kenkyu*" (A Study of the Problems in Education), two that were published in educational journals. As recently as the late 1970s, ten volumes of the *Sawayanagi Masataro Zenshu* (*The Complete Works of Sawayanagi Masataro*) were published by Kodansha. As many theses as possible were collected from his original writings in *Ko/Shi Gakko Hikaku Ron* (*A Comparative Study of Private and Public Schools*), as well as from "*Jissaiteki Kyoikugaku*" (Practical Pedagogy), an essay outlining his pedagogical views.

The *Complete Works* begins with "*Jissaiteki Kyoikugaku*," which includes writings concerning Sawayanagi's theories of moral training, the state, pedagogy, and the study of teachers. The seventh volume of the *Complete Works*, entitled *Shukyo to Kyoiku* (*Religion and Education*), is particularly important for an understanding of Sawayanagi's Buddhist thought, which is considered to have had a great influence on his educational theory. The eighth and ninth volumes, entitled *Sekai no Naka no Nihon no Kyoiku* (*Japanese Education Within the World*), which take as background the changes in the educational and historical conditions in both Asian and western countries, analyzes how Japanese education should be conducted. This study labels Sawayanagi an international educator.

Apart from the *Complete Works, Bek-kan—Sawayanagi Masataro Kenkyu (An Additional Study of Masataro Sawayanagi)* has also been published. A bibliography of Sawayanagi's studies and representative domestic articles are included in this volume, indispensable for those who wish to research Sawayanagi's accomplishments within the New Movement in Education. An explanatory text at the end of each volume not only contains comments on the articles but also includes independent studies by young Japanese scholars that provide a unique perspective on Sawayanagi's life.

When Sawayanagi was actively engaged in his various educational endeavors, Japanese society was experiencing instability and unrest, even though the nation had made considerable progress in the fields of politics, economics, and culture. According to Sawayanagi, Japan's rapid modernization since the Meiji Restoration of 1868 had been achieved as a result of the government and the people working together toward the accomplishment of the nation's "Four Great Tasks." These included: (1) a revision of the unequal treaties signed at the opening of the country to the West, which placed Japan in a disadvantageous relationship with western countries; (2) the establishment of a modern political system, including the adoption of a constitutional form of government and a system of local government; (3) an expansion of the economic and military power of the nation, which had been weakened after the Sino-Japanese War (1894–95), the Russo-Japanese War (1904–5), and the annexation of Korea (1910); and (4) an improvement in the general cultural level of the Japanese in order to achieve equality with western cultures. Sawayanagi believed that the accomplishment of the Four Great Tasks contributed greatly to national solidarity as Japan struggled to gain status with other world powers.

Sawayanagi thought, however, that the period following the completion of the Tasks was marked by instability despite the rapid progress and advancements Japan had made. The country still faced international isolation on one hand and, on the other, the loss of a national aim for unity, both of which brought on social unrest. Sawayanagi concluded that "outwardly the country became an object of envy but inwardly the people's spirit had deteriorated." He warned that "it is very dangerous to depend upon diplomacy and military expansion in order to cope with the difficulties of the state." He recognized that at that time "the difficulties of the state were unprecedented in the history of Japan."

Sawayanagi insisted that Japan had committed serious mistakes as a nation by resorting to violence through military expansion, and that the only way to avoid that danger was to promote education and culture. This approach formed the foundation of Sawayanagi's advocacy of the establishment of a state based on education. He believed that the power of education itself could bring prosperity to a nation.

Sawayanagi placed little emphasis on national prosperity in material terms such as the increase in productivity, but instead emphasized the advancement of spiritual and cultural aspects of the society. He considered these elements to be indispensable to Japan's modernization, particularly since the country possessed few raw materials and lagged behind western countries in industrial productivity. And even if Japan's productivity matched that of western countries, Sawayanagi was convinced that Japan would still be inferior spiritually and culturally. In any event, the development of education would be essential for the spiritual and cultural advancement of the nation.

Sawayanagi's brand of nationalism was based on the doctrine that the enhancement of the state was dependent on education, through which the enlightenment of the people could be carried out. In order to raise the educational levels of the masses, Sawayanagi felt that the fulfillment of primary education would make it possible for the people to be educated in common, without regard to sex, wealth, or family background. The foundation of the Seijo Elementary School, then, represented the realization of his educational ideal in its experimental form.

Sawayanagi's principle of the advancement of the state dependent on education was grounded on his expectations of the potential of children as human beings and citizens. In other words, the greater the crisis faced by society, the more it depended on its youth to eventually overcome the obstacles. This can be seen in Sawayanagi's thoughts during this period of crisis in Japanese capitalism, the result of remarkable progress in the face of internal contradictions and the possible mobilization of the people for an "Imperial war."

It seemed essential to Sawayanagi that educational and cultural differences among the various regions of Japan be abolished in order to promote a nationalism dependent on education and to balance development between urban and rural culture. To improve the level of rural culture, Sawayanagi, utilizing the example of England, insisted upon the necessity of educational institutions, such as local universities, that were isolated from urban areas and therefore far from the concentration of politics and commercial power. For example, this principle was implemented during his term of office at the Ministry of Education when he established new higher normal schools such as the Nara Higher Normal School for Women (now Nara Women's University) and the Hiroshima Higher Normal School (now Hiroshima University). This was a great step forward, since the two new schools were not located in one of the major Japanese cities at that time, such as Tokyo, Osaka, or Kyoto.

Sawayanagi the educator, thinker, and government official exhibited both an international and national perspective. First of all, like most advocates of modernization of the day, Sawayanagi regarded western countries as "advanced," considering it important for Japan to learn from them in order to achieve equality within international society. Having visited western countries on four occasions, Sawayanagi upon his return could always be found comparing trends in western culture and education with those of Japan, vigorously emphasizing the path Japanese education should follow and the essential philosophy its policies should be based upon. At the same time Sawayanagi criticized the habit of worshiping all things western, emphasizing the adoption of things Asian for educational and diplomatic policies. To him, modernization clearly did not entail complete devotion to westernization.

Sawayanagi's "Asianism" emphasized a Japanese initiative among Asian countries. He explained that "if the conditions in other Asian countries are so pitiful, then our country should help them improve." In addition, he had a clear opinion about "white aggression in the East"—that is, colonialism. Sawayanagi wrote that "our country has the responsibility of sweeping away white aggression from Asia." His intent was to develop Asian culture and to intensify the solidarity of Asian nations, yet he could not avoid justifying Japanese economic and military intervention in other Asian countries. He stated: "The Japanese people should maintain their status among the world powers with the mission of displaying Japan's power as the leading nation in the East." He reasoned that "since the population of our country will increase by several hundred thousand every year, Japan must inevitably expand into foreign countries sometime in the future" (1916).

Initially he was unaware of the significance of national independence or self-determination movements, considering Japanese military involvement such as the Sino-Japanese War and the Russo-Japanese War inevitable. He called for the people's "resolution and preparedness" and stated that "we must expand our national power into Korea and Manchuria." In retrospect, we realize that he could not have understood or appreciated the nationalist anticolonial movements among Asian countries or the anti–Japanese imperialist campaign against the annexation of Korea in 1910. Although he was considered an advocate of Japanese imperialism, his earlier attitudes toward Asia and the world were inconsistent with those of his later years. When he emphasized the urgent necessity of "remodeling the nation" by education, he expected education to contribute to the "fulfillment of the Japanese Empire despite the difficult diplomatic relations Japan faced in order to achieve recognition within the international community." Such an attitude would have been severely criticized as imperialistic, but because of his virtues, such as humility and modesty, Sawayanagi was also considered a democrat.

Sawayanagi traveled to the West on an inspection trip from August 1921 to the summer of the following year, after a period of fifteen years in Japan. During the eleven months traveling throughout Europe, he observed the ruins left by World War I. He felt that the destruction in Europe, however, was nothing compared with that caused by the Sino-Japanese War or the

Russo-Japanese War. This tour finally convinced him that Japan had no choice but to develop itself through education and culture, not by military power. The trip was of great significance in the sense that it directed his thinking toward democratic progressive education.

Sawayanagi concluded that "the more democratic the society becomes, the more significant the function of elementary education becomes." But his understanding, reinforced by the western trip, gave him new insights concerning social progress. He admitted that before his trip he had believed that society was divided into three classes—upper, middle, and lower—and that "the driving forces of the world lay mainly in the hands of the middle class." After the trip, he confessed a change of mind: "I came to the conclusion that the masses constitute the nucleus of society." Therefore, he claimed in an article entitled "The Significance of Education" (October 1922) that he had come to feel strongly about the importance of mass elementary education. In addition, he emphasized the importance of women's education, of adult and workers' education, of reducing the numbers of students per class, of equal opportunity in education, and of bettering teachers' working conditions.

One of the most important characteristics of Sawayagi's educational views is his understanding of history concerning the issues of progress and development. For example, the rapid progress of culture and education in the early Meiji era (the latter part of the nineteenth century) was attributed not only to the introduction and application of western culture; rather, Sawayanagi observed that in the history of Japanese culture and mass education before the Meiji Restoration, a solid foundation had been laid that made possible the rapid modernization during the subsequent Meiji period. Therefore, he emphasized that the positive aspects of earlier Japanese culture, customs, and traditions should be recognized along with those from the West in contributing to Japan's modernization. Without both, he thought, modernization would not root itself deeply in Japanese soil.

Sawayanagi especially appreciated the writings of Kaibara Eikiken (1630–1714), a scholar of natural history and one of the more prominent figures who followed the doctrines of Chu Tzu.

In Kaibara's time, education was considered necessary only for the upper classes. In contrast, Kaibara had insisted that "all people, even those in the social classes below that of the samurai, should be educated from childhood." It was this progressive concept that attracted Sawayanagi to Kaibara's thinking.

In addition, Kaibara's thought concerning methods of teaching appealed to Sawayanagi. Kaibara believed that children's play derives from nature, which should not be oppressed. In the child's observation of the world, Kaibara had developed the idea of the psychological growth of the child from the philosophy of Chu Tzu. Sawayanagi praised it highly, stating: "I was deeply impressed with Kaibara's foresight in calling for education appropriate to the child's natural growth both in mind and body." In Kaibara's *Wazoku Doshi Kun* (*Disciplinary Education for Japanese Children*), the main principles concerning the content and method of education were included under the title *Zuinen Kyoho* (*Yearly Teachings*), which could be considered the beginning of the modern view of children with its concern for the natural "yearly" growth of the child. Some contemporary Japanese scholars of educational history consider this book to be the first definitive work on educational theory in Japanese history. Sawayanagi called Kaibara the John Locke of Japan.

Sawayanagi thus focused his attention on earlier Japanese figures such as Kaibara as the foundation that made possible the rapid development of modern education in Japan. He constructed his views regarding children's education and the concept of their growth upon the ideas of historical thinkers. He also evaluated highly the mass education offered by the *shijuku* (small private classes) and *terakoya* (temple schools) widely organized during the Edo period. According to Sawayanagi, the success of the private classes and schools showed that "ordinary people had respect for learning and instruction, spontaneously providing opportunities for education without governmental assistance." He explained that these traditional practices paved the way for "modern education" and "exercised an indirect influence on its early development."

The spread of educational provisions in private schools and classes of an earlier period stimulated the Taisho New Movement in Education to aim at reducing school and classroom numbers in order to restore close human relations between teachers and students. Characteristic of this reform was the tendency to return to the traditional ways of education offered by the old temple schools, the *terakoya*, of which the main curriculum was the repeated practice of the "three R's" along with disciplinary training. It is clear that Sawayanagi's evaluation of the *terakoya* as a foundation for modern Japanese education made a significant impact on the growth of the Taisho New Movement in Education. It is here that one can witness the genesis of the ideas that later were carried out at the Seijo Elementary School.

As mentioned before, under the surge of the New Movement of Education, Sawayanagi founded the Seijo Elementary School and was inaugurated as the first principal in April 1917, at the age of fifty-one. He quickly found that his duties as principal were all-consuming. The establishment and administration of the Seijo Elementary School, in fact, signified the conclusion of his educational activities and studies.

With the opening of the school, Sawayanagi directed his attention to hiring the most competent and talented teachers from all over the country. The school advertised publicly for teachers, an unusual procedure. About fifty candidates responded. In selecting the new teachers, Sawayanagi requested the submission of a paper on "The Story of My Life." One of the reasons for requesting such a paper was to judge the literary ability of each candidate. They were also asked a variety of other questions, such as: Do you like children? Do you like to read? Write the names of books other than the ones on education that you have read and the reasons why you have chosen them. Are you good at talking with children? This unusual method of screening new teachers, rather than the traditional test of knowledge of information, was indicative of the school's fresh approach to education.

Sawayanagi emphasized that successful education depended upon the ability of teachers and their efforts to develop their own characters. These concepts were central to many of his writings concerning teachers, such as "The Teacher and the Principal" (1908) and "The Spirit of an Educator" (1895). Furthermore, he attached much importance to love and compassion toward children by the teacher and declared that these qualities are as important as intellect. He said, "A good teacher loves children. Those who do not should not teach."

"The hopes and ideals of the school" were vividly expressed in his widely distributed Prospectus on the Establishment of the Seijo Elementary School. The following are a few notable items: (1) education respecting individuality; (2) education respecting nature; (3) education respecting feelings; and (4) education based on scientific analysis.

When the school was finally opened in Tokyo, it had seven teachers, with Sawayanagi acting as principal, and thirty-five pupils—twenty-eight in the first grade and seven in the second grade. It adopted a unique method for admission. Two opportunities to enter the school were offered, one in the spring and the other in autumn; consequently a dual grading system was adopted. Although the number of pupils gradually increased with the development of the school's reputation, the maximum capacity of each classroom was maintained at below thirty students in order to emphasize individual education for the pupils. This contrasted sharply with the public elementary-school classroom of the day, with as many as seventy students enrolled in one class.

The teachers of Sawayanagi's school pursued their studies on education with enthusiasm. For instance, Yamashita Tokuharu (1892–1965), a teacher at the school beginning in 1920, was an industrious man who read 3,000 pages a month on average from such works as *Asu no Gakkō* (*School for Tomorrow*) as well as in the fields of philosophy, literature, social sciences, and natural sciences, including writings and articles in foreign languages. Sawayanagi and his colleagues recognized this man's attributes by providing him with the opportunity to study at a German university for five years. He was the first from the school to study abroad.

We can see one aspect of the energetic efforts of the teachers in the "inter-class joint research" that resulted in the establishment of a "normal school" within the school. This research was organized across the boundaries of subjects as a seminar on self-motivated education. Sessions for the teachers were held for two hours each day after the regular classes at Seijo. Auditors from outside the school were also allowed to attend the classes. The results of the teachers' research activities were published in their journal *Kyoiku Mondai Kenkyu* (*Study of Educational Problems*). From the first issue in April 1920 to August 1921, when he left for the West, Sawayanagi contributed to nearly every issue. Each of his articles not only had an impact on the educational world of Japan but in the process brought more prestige to the school.

A number of other books by Sawayanagi and his colleagues at the school were also published. For example, *A Critical Study of the Dalton Plan* (1923–24) introduced this famous method to Japan through its use at the Seijo School. This individualized method of learning, in which learning material was arranged in a number of assignments and the student signed a "contract" to complete each assignment, was made famous by Helen Parkhurst through her book *Education of the Dalton Plan*, published in 1922. Miss Parkhurst was invited to Japan by the Seijo School.

Although the quality of the teachers at the school was extraordinary, Seijo Elementary School was best known within the New Movement in Education for its unique methods in education. Sawayanagi was considered the most important leader in the movement. The innovations that he and his colleagues introduced at the school include the following:

- Ethical teachings taught from the fourth grade.
- Arithmetic taught from the second grade.
- History and geography taught from the fourth grade.
- An aural communication course.
- A dramatics course.
- Educational films.
- The study of juvenile literature.
- The Dalton Plan.
- Correlation between drawing and handicraft instruction.

All of these were put into practice, with special attention being focused on whether the subject offered fit the natural growth level of the child. Sawayanagi insisted from the school's earliest days that much more attention should be paid to the "grading of a subject"—that is, its proper grade level in relation to the student's growth—and criticized contemporary pedagogy that considered only subject matter. In *Practical Pedagogy* he stated that the grade level corresponding to the level of the pupil's growth should be carefully examined. Such practices attracted considerable public response.

Generally speaking, before World War II, the elementary-school curriculum was strictly controlled by the government. In most cases teachers found it difficult to exhibit creativity in their teaching or in the organization of their materials. They functioned simply as intermediaries in presenting the material prescribed by the government. In these conditions, the educational policies of Seijo Elementary School played a role of historical significance as the first major education experiment within a private school relatively free from centralized governmental control. Prior to Sawayanagi's work at Seijo School, virtually no attempts at innovation in elementary-school content had been carried out. The Seijo experiment was consequently the first challenge to the structure of the established curriculum in all subjects.

Sawayanagi and his colleagues were also concerned with the appropriate class size for school education and the propriety of coeducation. They discussed how to guide children according to their individual differences based on their rate of growth, a most novel idea at that time. Other innovations included new methods in teaching English. For example, Harold Palmer, the well-known American scholar of English linguistics, was invited to Japan by the school. The so-called Palmer Method had already achieved some notoriety in America. Bringing the founder of the new method to Japan was an indication of Sawayanagi's progressive nature.

The theory and methods Sawayanagi and his colleagues introduced at the Seijo Elementary School underlay both his systematic theory of practical pedagogy and the concept of child-centered education. The former, Sawayanagi emphasized, was based on the goal of developing the teacher's independent creative attitude toward teaching. The latter emphasized the use of pedagogy to educate children in the proper manner. We can find the essence of Sawayanagi's theory of education in the harmony between practical pedagogy and child-centered education.

Sawayanagi summarized his basic attitudes toward the educational practices at the Seijo School by stating, "We focus our eyes upon children. Everything we do at the school originates from that point." This was, of course, in contrast to the teacher- or subject-centered instruction in the classrooms of Japan. He emphasized that the child should be recognized as the "lord of learning" by saying that "the context of education must be seen from the perspective of those who are to be educated—that is, the children."

Sawayanagi never wavered in his conviction that the new school should integrate the concepts of child-centered instruction and the systematic combination of school subjects. What made his thinking so progressive can best be understood by reflecting on the prevailing attitude toward the classroom in Japan. Before Sawayanagi appeared on the scene, public-school classrooms had been dominated by the teaching approach advocated by the German philosopher Johann Friedrich Herbart with his formalistic five-step teaching method. The typical Japanese class was characterized by rote memorization, drill, repetition, and testing.

The significance of Sawayanagi's position in the historical context of Japanese education lies in his emphasis on the individuality and spontaneity of children, and his bitter criticism of the formalism of Japanese schools. What is most fascinating about his position is that his criticism began with the subject of *shushin* (ethics or morals). Since the 1880s *shushin* had been given the highest rank among all school subjects. Based on the precepts contained in the Imperial Rescript on Education, *shushin* was considered the core of the school curriculum, that which molded the Japanese child into a proper Japanese citizen. It taught children how a Japanese subject should show loyalty to the Emperor and to his or her family. Therefore, criticizing the content and method of *shushin* bordered on blasphemy. The fact that Sawayanagi initiated his attack on the schools of the day with severe criticism of *shushin* rendered him one of the most prominent leaders of the New Movement in Education.

Although Sawayanagi made an indelible mark on the history of progressive education in Japan, and is remembered today as the distinguished educator who founded the liberal private Seijo

School, his importance to Japanese education extends far beyond that accomplishment. His role as Vice Minister of Education, the top professional post in the Ministry of Education, as well as his presidency of two of the leading national universities—a fact that is little remembered today—makes him perhaps the only Japanese educator ever to function in such a broad spectrum of activities. At each level he made a distinctive contribution.

The real uniqueness of the man, however, lies in the evolution of his educational thought and practice away from traditional public education, with its uniformity and standardization and its state-centered morality at the foundation. The emergence of the Seijo School, with its radical principles of progressive education, marked his complete transformation from the traditionalist to the liberalist. It is from this perspective that Sawayanagi deserves recognition as one of the greatest educators to have come from Japan.

The Life of Sawayanagi Masataro

1865   Born in Matsumoto City, Nagano Prefecture.
1875   Moved to Tokyo; entered elementary school attached to the Tokyo Normal School.
1884   Entered Tokyo University.
1888   Entered the Ministry of Education.
1892   Resigned from the Ministry; became principal of a middle school in Kyoto.
1895   Became principal of a middle school in Gumma; published *The Spirit of an Educator*.
1898   Became principal of the First National Higher School.
1906   Appointed Vice Minister of Education.
1908   Published *The Teacher and the Principal* and *Method of Learning*.
1910   Published *Education of our Nation, Morals for Girls*, and *Filial Piety*.
1911   Appointed President, Tohoku Imperial University.
1913   Appointed President, Kyoto Imperial University.

1914 Forced to resign from Kyoto Imperial University.
1916 Became principal of the new Seijo Middle School; elected President of the Imperial Education Society (Teikoku Kyoiku Kai).
1917 Established Seijo Elementary School and became the principal.
1921 Traveled to Europe to observe educational practices.
1926 Established Seijo High School and became the principal.
1927 Died on December 24.

About the Author

Hiroshi Mizuuchi was born in 1939 in Niigata Prefecture, and graduated in 1964 from the University of Tokyo's Faculty of Education. He joined the faculty of Tsuru Bunka University in 1968, and completed the doctoral course at the University of Tokyo in 1969. He is currently Assistant Professor at Chiba University. His publications (in Japanese) include *Japanese Education during World War I* (1976) and *Reconstruction of Elementary Education* (1979).

Shimonaka Yasaburo in his later years.

Shimonaka Yasaburo

[1878-1961]

Akira Nakano

Shimonaka Yasaburo is most prominently known in Japan as the prewar founder of Heibonsha, one of the major publishing houses in Japan and best known for its encyclopedias and art books. He is also remembered as a pacifist who devoted himself to the cause of world peace in the postwar era by denouncing the production and testing of nuclear weapons by both the United States and the Soviet Union. Shimonaka thus led a very active life right up until his death at the age of eighty-three. Even in January of the year of his death, 1961, he sent a letter to President John F. Kennedy in response to his State of the Union message. The President's warning that if mankind did not annihilate war, war would annihilate mankind motivated Shimonaka to sit down and write a personal letter to the President of the United States applauding his speech and calling for the destruction of all nuclear arms. President Kennedy replied that the letter from abroad was most encouraging. Shimonaka, who was deeply moved by the response from the young American president, died shortly thereafter.

Few Japanese are aware of Shimonaka's background as a teacher both in a local primary school and in a normal school before the war. In fact, he was in the vanguard of the first left-wing teachers' movement in prewar Japan. He also wrote several books and many articles on education. In 1974, more than ten years after his death, his writings were compiled and published under the title *Bannin Rodo no Kyoiku (Education for All Workers)*. With this publication, interest in the life of the man was rekindled after a period of relative obscurity. Some would say that Shimonaka, as a great Japanese educator, had been a "forgotten man" in the postwar era.

Shimonaka Yasaburo was born in the mountain village of Tate-kui, Hyogo Prefecture—nestled amid the Chugoku mountains—in the year 1878, exactly ten years after the Meiji Restoration. Tatekui was a tiny farming settlement. Since the average size of the farms was so small, the local people could not survive on farming alone, and many turned to making pottery from the abundant clay deposits in the area to eke out a living. Shimonaka was brought up in such a family: a half-farmer, half-potter household.

The young boy lost his father at the age of two, which cast the family into further financial straits. Shimonaka was thus forced to quit school at the third-grade level in order to help with the family work for survival. Ironically, these trying circumstances came to play a vital role in his life. He never lost sight of his humble beginnings in rural Japan.

A local elementary-school teacher took pity on this hardworking lad by offering to teach him in the evenings after he had completed his daily work. A neighborhood doctor, also recognizing the keenness of the boy, allowed him to freely use his personal books and dictionaries. Slowly, Shimonaka began the long and painful process of educating himself through the kindness of these neighbors. He also gained a measure of self-confidence upon the success of his pottery skills, developing a highly regarded local technique.

These experiences as a young boy growing up in an impoverished area of Japan during the late 1800s came to have a profound influence on Shimonaka as he founded his publishing house many years later. He often wrote on the importance to every working person of continuing to learn. Of the greatest importance to him—in fact, basic to education—was learning by oneself, the self-taught principle. To learn was every individual's right regardless of position. Society was responsible to provide the proper environment to accomplish this. One of his major purposes in launching a publishing house that became synonymous with encyclopedias was to provide every individual with the essential books for educating himself.

In 1897, at the age of nineteen, Shimonaka moved to Kobe,

Shimonaka with other members of the faculty of the Japan Women's School of Fine Arts, 1904.

Staff of *Women's News*, 1906. Shimonaka is seated in the center.

Shimonaka (center of the photograph) with faculty and students of the
Saitama Prefectural Normal School, ca. 1914.

With his family, ca. 1925.

where he was taken on as an assistant teacher of a primary school, even though he himself had never completed primary school. His work at the school inspired him to independently study the discipline of pedagogy more deeply. He then applied for the position as a regular teacher and was able to pass the examination for the appointment as full-time elementary-school teacher.

Then, in 1902, he came to Tokyo seeking a new outlet for his energies. With his experiences as a local schoolteacher and his growing interest in broader social issues, he was able to start a small newspaper for children. This marks his initial step into the publishing business. Shortly thereafter he expanded his enterprise by circulating the *Fujin Shimbun*, a newspaper designed for women readers.

The new publishing interest came at a time of great moment in the history of the nation. The most notable event was the Russo-Japanese War of 1904–5, which had overwhelming public support. There were pockets of opposition, nevertheless, but they were drowned out in the outburst of nationalistic support of the war effort. Shimonaka was also caught up in the spirit of the time in which a small nation like Japan rose up against the aggression of Imperial Russia.

At the same time Shimonaka was torn between his nationalistic feelings and his pacifist emotions. He recognized the great tragedy of war. He took the bold step of submitting a poem entitled "Long Live the Devil" to the newspaper *Heimin Shimbun*, issued by a group of Japanese socialists, in which he mocked the cause of war. He described the great Japanese victory over Russia as a "victory for the Devil" on the road toward the destruction of humankind.

Shortly thereafter Shimonaka isolated himself in a tiny straw-thatched hut located away from the hustle and bustle of Tokyo. He devoted himself to the study of Asian philosophy and thought, particularly that of Confucius. This style of life was in sharp contrast to that of the socialists, for whom he had expressed sympathy shortly before. In virtual seclusion from the real world, he pondered the problems of man and how society should cope with the problems of the times. It was through this experience that he developed the concept of social reform by means of individual spiritual reformation.

At that time Shimonaka became engrossed with two figures, Saigo Takamori of Japan and Mahatma Gandhi of India. These two great statesmen and national leaders attracted Shimonaka's attention because of their common unselfish interest in the poor and destitute and their struggles to promote a national identity. In order to restore Japan to the position of a moral nation, Shimonaka concluded that the spirit of Saigo and Gandhi should pervade contemporary Japanese people. Without such a conversion, a spiritual reformation of the society could not be achieved.

By the year 1911, Shimonaka had decided to pursue a teaching career. Accordingly, he gained an appointment to the faculty of the Saitama Prefectural Normal School as a specialist in pedagogy. The aim of public normal schools of that period was to train teachers for the Imperial state in accordance with the principles stipulated in the Normal School Order promulgated by Mori Arinori, the first Minister of Education, in 1886.

All normal-school students were required to live in dormitories. They underwent a militaristic-type training course in some ways similar to the training of an army recruit. The products of a teacher-training college were consequently referred to as "normal-school types," implying rather accurately that they were fanatic nationalists. They were imbued with the dogma associated with an imperial state.

Shimonaka turned out to be a most unusual faculty member of a normal school. Above all, he despised the formalism and bureaucratic atmosphere of these government-run teacher-training institutions. For example, all students in the dormitories were required to stand in formation each morning while the head of the dormitory, a live-in faculty member, issued instructions on the rigid dormitory life. A student living in Shimonaka's dormitory recalled the experience:

> We always thought of morning ceremony as the time when the head of the dormitory would berate the students for their improper behavior. Mr. Shimonaka never did this, however. In fact, he followed the practice of speaking to us each morning while sitting quietly on the back of an old wooden horse located at the edge of the grounds.
>
> One morning he sat on the horse in meditation for a very

long time. We gazed at him in wonder. Had he forgotten
what he was supposed to talk about? He finally broke the
silence with the words: "The flowers and buds of the trees
are bursting forth into the heavens. The spirit of youth is
like that." He then quietly walked away without uttering
another word. We were astonished.

Shimonaka handled his classroom in a similar unconventional
manner. It was a firmly established principle that normal-school
teachers taught their classes strictly adhering to the textbooks
approved by the Ministry of Education. According to one student's vivid recollection, the atmosphere of Shimonaka's classroom was decidedly abnormal:

> His teaching method was most unique to us. First of all,
> he never used the official textbook. In fact, he rarely brought
> any material with him when he gave his lectures. One day,
> however, he brought in a book with a beautiful cover. It
> was the novel *Nihyaku-toka* [*A Stormy Day*], written by Na-
> tsume Soseki, the famous writer.
> Shimonaka, with a neatly cropped mustache and wearing
> glasses, was dressed in a fine striped suit. In a quiet but rich
> voice, which stood in sharp contrast to the rather cynical
> readings of the regular teachers of Japanese, he read from
> the novel during class for the next several days. We were
> all deeply moved by it.

As these recollections indicate, Shimonaka was an appealing
teacher to his students. He had a great deal of confidence in
them as well, treating them like human beings. He respected
their individuality by encouraging a sense of spontaneity and
the ability to think independently. Among his fellow teachers
he was considered a virtual heretic, all the more so because he
continually endeavored to become a better teacher.

An incident that took place upon the death of Emperor Meiji
in 1912 illustrates the character of Shimonaka. The great general
Nogi Maresuke and his wife, on hearing of the death of the Emperor, committed ritual suicide as a final act of loyalty. The
incident created a great controversy, with many people praising

the general and his wife for their unselfish devotion to their ruler, while some intellectuals criticized the actions as misguided devotion.

On the occasion, an art teacher at the Saitama Normal School gave his students the assignment of making a bust of General Nogi out of plaster. Eight of the students turned in eight virtually identical busts, which were obviously copies. When the faculty met to discuss the appropriate punishment, Shimonaka opposed any action against the students. He claimed that it was the fault not of the students but of the institution itself, which compelled every student to take every course, including art, whether they had an interest in the subject or not. His opinion was overruled. It was trying for Shimonaka to continue teaching at the normal school, which paid so little attention to the individuality of the students.

During this period Shimonaka prepared a *nichijo hyakka sho jiten*, a daily handbook. He called it *Kore wa Benri Da!* (*Oh, That's Handy!*). He explained the origin of it in the following way:

> During the early days of the Taisho era, when I was a teacher at the Saitama Normal School, I came up with a new idea while going over some examination papers. I was shocked at the students' lack of literary knowledge and their careless manner in writing. Therefore I lectured them on composition and their use of grammar and the proper meaning of words. Somehow it motivated an interest among the students, who were really quite poor in writing answers to test questions, contrary to what I had expected from aspiring teachers.
>
> I met with the manager of a publishing company, who encouraged me to compile a book of current usage and grammar. He reacted to my explanation by saying that such a publication would be "very handy." From that I derived the name *Oh, That's Handy!* for my little handbook.

Oh, That's Handy! was in fact the beginning of the Heibonsha Publishing Company. The original publisher went bankrupt. This prompted Shimonaka to set up a new publishing company in name only in order to continue the publication of his hand-book. When he asked his wife what kind of a name he should give his new publishing outfit, she replied simply that it should be an "ordinary name." He promptly called it Heibonsha, lit-erally an "ordinary" (*heibon*) company (*-sha*). From that humble beginning Heibonsha developed into the great publishing house of today.

Upon the launching of his new business in 1915, Shimonaka resigned as a full-time faculty member of the Saitama Normal School to devote his energies to his new company. Nevertheless he continued on the faculty as a part-time teacher for the next three years. In 1918, he entered into a new period in his life and one which was to have a long-term influence on the educational world of Japan that has continued to this very day.

Just six years previously, Emperor Taisho had succeeded to the throne upon the death of Emperor Meiji in 1912. During those few years a remarkable movement to democratize Japa-nese politics and society had gotten under way. For example, when Prime Minister Saionji Kinmochi, a comparatively liberal politician, was forced to resign over a conflict with military au-thorities, a popular movement developed in protest. Literally tens of thousands of citizens took to the streets to demonstrate their opposition to the right-wing politicians who were installed in the new cabinet.

The opposition, however, ultimately reached a level sufficient to bring about the downfall of the new government. The event is noted in Japanese history as one of considerable moment in which the general populace for the first time played a leading role in bringing about political change. It is even referred to as the Taisho Political Crisis (Taisho Seihen), implying that a new order in the national arena of Japanese politics had taken place.

A variety of spontaneous activities subsequently took place. For example, a movement of workers led by an association called the Yūaikai (Friendship Society) spread throughout the land under the leadership of Suzuki Bunji, a Christian humanist. An article written by Yoshino Sakuzo, a professor at the preeminent Tokyo Imperial University, in the widely read journal *Chuo Koron* attracted widespread attention. Under the title "An Essay on the

Basic Principles of Constitutional Government," this distinguished authority on labor problems called for a democratic form of government in Japan. He argued persuasively that although the Emperor was specifically designated the supreme ruler in the Constitution, the actual implementation of governmental power should be based on a national consensus.

Gradually the term *democracy* began to infiltrate writings on education. The great educational reformer Sawayanagi Masataro used the term in his well-known article "Comment on Democracy." He claimed that those who despise democracy eulogize absolutism and support bureaucracy. Sawayanagi's opinions had much influence in the world of education, since he himself was a former Vice Minister of Education and had held the presidency of two Imperial universities. In addition, his writings were given great prominence because he was the president of the Teikoku Kyoikukai, the Imperial Society of Education, which included all of the public-school teachers of the land.

At this time, right after World War I, the average Japanese lived a very difficult life. Although a few people had become rich on the spoils of war, most people were poverty-stricken. They resented the nouveaux-riches. Rice riots in Toyama Prefecture quickly spread to other areas of the country as popular opposition movements expanded their activities.

Teachers suffered as much as workers and farmers, with sharp increases in inflation producing a ripple effect throughout the economy. During the period prior to 1918, while the cost of living doubled, teachers' salaries remained constant. An educational magazine of the period commented, "Even though teaching is considered a sacred profession, teachers are only human. Under the conditions they face, it is only natural that they express their deep dissatisfaction. Listen to their weak voices desperately calling out from every classroom, 'I cannot find a way out. I must quit teaching. I cannot continue to live this way.' These are voices of our teachers."

Under these conditions, teachers began searching for new ways to protect their livelihood. Accordingly, Shimonaka together with his followers launched a movement that, in retrospect, was of enormous significance. They set out to organize a new group called Keimeikai (simply, Enlightened Society) in

August of 1919, and published the following declaration of intent at the outset:

> Our ideal is to attain a just life based upon human rights. We recognize the basic rights of human beings and respect their inalienable social rights.
>
> We are Japanese. We assert our sincerity as Japanese citizens and our desire to be loyal to the just and great principles of our country. Therefore we reject all irrational and unnatural laws, conventions, and thought contrary to these principles.
>
> We are educators. We are conscious of our vocation and will devote ourselves to the education of all people.

The purpose of the new movement was centered specifically on the improvement of the life of the classroom teacher through improvement in teachers' salaries and their status in general. However, there was a much larger purpose behind Shimonaka's efforts. This was an attempt at nothing less than social reformation through the instrument of the schools. To the leaders of this quite radical movement at the time, it was indispensable that the school become free from outside—namely, government—interference.

The new organization began publishing a periodical called *Keimei (Enlightenment)* in order to spread its message on a broader scale. As the guiding figure within the movement, Shimonaka contributed a series of articles expressing his viewpoints. A year later his articles were compiled under one cover and published in book form as *Kyoiku Saizo (The Reconstruction of Education)*.

During the year 1920, Keimeikai leaders stepped up their activities. In a bold move, Keimeikai joined a group of progressive organizations to officially sponsor the first public May Day celebrations ever held in Japan, at Ueno Park in Tokyo. The national newspapers reported that Shimonaka spoke to the crowd with great emotion, criticizing the inequality of the schools and calling for a national system of education that provided for equal educational opportunities for all. Keimeikai, broadening its concern far beyond the classroom, presented a motion demanding an immediate withdrawal of all Japanese military forces from

Soviet Siberia, the abolition of press control, and the complete financing of education at public expense. For the occasion, Shimonaka had written a song entitled simply "A Song for May Day."

In September, the name Keimeikai was expanded to Nihon Kyoin Kumiai Keimeikai (The Japan Teachers' Union Enlightened Association). The reason for the name change related to the increasingly progressive attitude of the leaders in their endeavor to strengthen the solidarity between teachers and workers. As the first union of teachers in Japanese history, the newly named organization plunged into the expanding labor movement.

The union, under the influence of Shimonaka, issued a four-point declaration for the educational reconstruction of Japanese schools:

I. The Ideals of Education in Society
   1. We must develop modern culture on the basis of the spirit of the people in order to realize a just society.
   2. We must respect the spirit of labor and recognize that profligate living is a social sin.
   3. We must reject hostility among the people and promote love among all men, opposing bureaucratic intervention in our lives.
   4. In order to realize these aims both at home and abroad, we support the League of Nations and call for an International Congress on Education to promote international understanding and world peace.
II. Equal Educational Opportunities
   1. We recognize the right to learn as a human right. Therefore equality of educational opportunity should be provided as a social responsibility. We demand that a free education from the elementary-school level through the university be provided at public expense.
   2. Entry into secondary school should be based both on ability and desire. Secondary schools should be run on a half-day basis to enable students to participate in a variety of activities.
   3. Since university education would be provided at public

expense, the courses should be divided into required and elective categories. Elective courses should be open to the public without distinction based on age, sex, or prior knowledge. The university should also admit women on an equal basis with men.

III. The Autonomy of Education

1. In order to liberate education from bureaucratic control and to ensure the freedom of teachers, school administration should be organized by the teachers themselves.

2. A school board system, both locally and nationally, should be employed consisting of elected school representatives combined with appointed members from the academic, political, and governmental sectors, who would make up less than one-fourth of the total.

3. The school boards shall have the power to develop educational policy for the schools under their jurisdiction.

4. An independent organization of schoolteachers should be respected. Without such a union of teachers, the government will usurp the control of education from the teachers.

IV. The Organization of Education

1. We promote the organization of education that respects the growth of each individual child in the child-centered classroom.

2. We promote the abolition of the rigid grading system.

3. We promote the adaptation of the local school curriculum to the local environment of the community.

4. We promote the free selection of textbooks.

5. We promote the expansion of evening or part-time courses for older students.

These aims of the new teachers' union stem from Shimonaka's thoughts expressed in his writings that "all human beings have the right to life. When some people are starving, others do not have the right to live comfortable lives." He believed that progress of mankind evolved through the combined efforts of all people. However, he attributed the inequalities within societies to the immature evolution of the social structure. To Shimonaka, the evils of social inequality could be rectified through the influence of the school. The school to him should serve as an instrument to reform society.

Over and over again, and in a variety of ways, Shimonaka stood on the side of the poor in his demands for an equal opportunity of education. "Under the present system of education in Japan," he wrote, "only the better classes of society have the freedom to study. The poor must work for a living from an early age. Consequently they lose their freedom of study. In the process, children of the rich deprive the children of the poor of their opportunity to an equal education." This was the basis of his call for free public education for all at public expense and an end to all forms of discrimination in school.

Shimonaka argued that the national school system of Japan, inaugurated in 1872, derived from the initiative of the government rather than through the efforts of the public at large. The government leaders viewed a modern school system as a means to develop a rich country with a strong army. Therefore the government established certain obligations for each citizen in the form of taxation and military service. Thus, when Shimonaka claimed that education was a right of every citizen, it represented a unique ideal within the educational world at that time.

Shimonaka was also committed to international solidarity for world peace, as expressed in the principle of the Keimei union of teachers. In his book *Bannin Rodo no Kyoiku* (*Education for All Workers*), he wrote that human beings are sacrificed in the name of morality. In fact, the wealthy classes benefit from military aggression, while the victims are most often the poor. The privileged classes always gain materially from militarism.

The Russo-Japanese War was a good example. World War I also produced its share of Japanese who greatly profited from the spoils of war. In contrast, the public at large suffered under the steep rise in the cost of living and shortages caused by the war. Even at the time of his writing, Shimonaka claimed that many Japanese were living a desperate existence.

Shimonaka emphasized a relatively new concept in Japan, "peace education." Coming shortly after the end of World War I, it had a great impact on the educational world. In his campaign for the complete abolition of armaments, Shimonaka supported international campaigns and domestic education aimed at that goal. He claimed, "I am a patriot. I call for an unarmed Japan because I am a patriot." He firmly believed that world peace would come about through justice and faith among all people in the world, not through the buildup of military weaponry.

Keimeikai consequently vehemently opposed a bill presented by the government at that time to assign a military officer to each school for the purpose of conducting military drills with the students. Shimonaka attacked the measure, claiming that it would lead to the destruction of humane education. In spite of such opposition, the legislation was ultimately enacted and led Japanese education down the fatal militaristic road.

Among the four major recommendations promoted by Keimeikai, perhaps the most far-reaching proposals involved the popularly elected school board and the independent organization of teachers. Both measures were designed to achieve local autonomy of education. The local school board system was meant to protect local school administration from improper interference by the government. An independent teachers' organization, in contrast to the nationwide organization of teachers under government control, was meant to encourage teachers' local initiative.

The image of the teacher was of particular importance to Shimonaka. He once labeled the teacher as a laborer or worker (*rodosha*), implying that the classroom teacher was in effect a blue-collar worker similar to the factory worker. In an article written for the magazine *Kaiho* (*Liberation*) in 1921, he argued that the "teacher must recognize his social obligation and declare boldly that he is a laborer. He must then join hands with other workers."

An independent organization of teachers and a locally elected school board were both far too radical in the early 1920s to have any chance for actual implementation. Remarkably, both ideas were finally realized nearly thirty years later, during the great reforms of Japanese education carried out by the American Occupation authorities after World War II. This clearly demonstrates how far ahead of his time Shimonaka and his ideas for education reform actually were.

Shimonaka lived during the era of the 1920s when the so-called

New Movement in Education was under way both within Japan and abroad. He was a part of it through his participation in Kyoiku no Seikisha (Century of Education Society), which was established in 1923 to promote progressive movements in education. He actively supported the establishment of the experimental school Jido no Mura Shogakko (Children's Village Elementary School), located in Ikebukuro, Tokyo, one of a number of private progressive schools of the period.

At the same time Shimonaka took a strong interest in farmers' activities, calling farmers the "ethical producers." He became widely respected throughout the rural areas of Japan. During the 1920s and 1930s, Japanese agriculture was relegated to an inferior position as rapid industrialization took precedence. There were also severe crop losses as a result of natural occurrences. Farmers struggled against what seemed insurmountable problems.

Through the 1920s a considerable proportion of young military officers had been drawn from the ranks of rural Japan. As they grew more concerned with the plight of farmers, so did their resentment against the ruling civilian political classes. Right-wing fascism was growing apace in this fertile environment. Since Shimonaka had worked with farmers' movements for several years and had shown great sympathy for their struggles, he believed that these young military officers would cooperate with him in his efforts to overcome the crisis of the farmers.

As Japan plunged deeper and deeper into military conflict—first against China and finally against the United States and Britain—during the decade from 1931 to 1941, all opposition movements among socialists' and workers' organizations were suppressed by the fascist leaders who had gained control of the government. Those who had pressed for democracy in the 1920s struggled valiantly against the right-wing movements, but were eventually eliminated as an effective opposition. Japanese fascism finally ruled the country and set the direction of the nation until the bitter defeat in 1945.

It would have been natural to expect Shimonaka to play a leading role in the anti-fascist front in the 1930s. After all, he had been one of the major agitators for a democratic system of education in Japan for over a decade. However, Shimonaka abruptly left the democratic camp in the early 1930s and joined hands with the fascists in support of Japanese aggression. It was a remarkable transition that is difficult to fully comprehend or explain.

Shimonaka's change of attitude caused considerable controversy among his followers. Some of his journalist friends described him as a pendulum swinging back and forth. He himself said that he was a "lost pilgrim searching for the right way. I am what I always was: like a bamboo sprout, peeling off one layer of cover at a time." He never recognized his changes as a "conversion" from one position to the other as the political tides changed.

The fact cannot be denied, though, that this great liberalist of the 1920s became a champion of Japanese fascism and military aggression in the 1930s. However, in the intellectual history of Japan, we can see that Shimonaka's swing from the progressive to the extreme right was not an isolated case. Many of his contemporaries underwent a similar experience during the great transition from the Taisho Democracy of the 1920s to the Showa militarism of the 1930s, culminating in full-scale war in the 1940s.

Throughout both periods, nevertheless, there was one constant factor in Shimonaka's life. His attitude toward the Imperial system, which bordered on the edge of religious faith, never wavered. He was, in fact, a faithful worshiper of the Emperor. Even the progressive pronouncements of the left-wing Keimeikai were often preceded by the phrase "In obedience to His Majesty, the Emperor." He firmly believed in the eternal concept of Kokutai, the nation-state, with the Emperor at the center.

Shimonaka's interpretation of democracy even in the 1920s differed sharply from that of some of his left-wing friends. In particular, it was contrary to that of the communists, who advocated a revolutionary change of government. In contrast, Shimonaka's call for the democratization of the Japanese government meant within the Imperial system. It was never intended to exclude the Emperor as the central figure.

The fascist leaders of the 1930s exploited this traditional devotion to the Emperor by many if not most of the Japanese people. By using the pretext of serving the wishes of the Emperor, the militarists cleverly couched their aggression in terms of national and Imperial loyalty. Few Japanese, including Shimonaka, could foresee the horrible consequences of blindly following the radical right-wing governmental leaders who acted in the name of the Emperor. Shimonaka was led down the wrong road along with many of his contemporaries at all levels of the society.

Curiously, Shimonaka also paid much attention to the broader aspects of international developments. His support of the League of Nations through the Keimeikai's principles is a good example. However, behind this internationalism was a belief in Japanese superiority over other Asian peoples. He attacked western imperialism over Asian nations but later defended Japanese imperialism over the same peoples. Perhaps this prevalent way of thinking by many Japanese of the day was based on their desire to achieve equality with the very western nations they were criticizing. Therefore, when Japan invaded its Asian neighbors—most of whom were under the control of European powers—Shimonaka supported the action as a means of finally eliminating western colonialism in Asia.

During this period, Shimonaka's company, Heibonsha, developed into a major publishing house. He was able to effectively respond to the cultural desires of the Japanese people. His company issued a number of outstanding publications, including *A Complete Edition of the World of Art* in eighteen volumes, *A History of the French Revolution* in eight volumes, and *A World History of Drama* in six volumes. All of these greatly contributed to the cultural standards of Japan's publishing industry. The crowning achievement of Shimonaka in the publishing field was his epochal *Dai Hyakka Jiten* (*The Great Encyclopedia*), an unprecedented feat in publishing. Shimonaka wrote in the Foreword:

> I grew up virtually without the opportunity of receiving a regular school education. I had to learn almost exclusively from books. Because of this difficult experience as a youth, I decided to leave the teaching profession in order to enter the publishing field. From the very beginning I have longed to publish a fine encyclopedia comparable to those in the West. The French have *Larousse du XXième Siècle* and the Germans have *Meyer's Konversations Lexicon*. I hereby take great pleasure in declaring that the Japanese now have *The Great Encyclopedia*.

On August 15, 1945, Shimonaka was staying at a small mountain village in Yamanashi Prefecture when the Emperor announced over the radio that Japan had accepted the terms of the Potsdam Declaration. He was apparently shocked by the announcement. He had already lost one son in battle in the Philippines in May and another in a traffic accident at about the same time. Upon hearing the surrender announcement, he is reported to have said to a friend:

The surrender will deprive our country of much territory. But I truly believe our nation and our people will survive without losing hope. We will revive. I want to devote the rest of my life to the cause of world peace through publications related to education. I believe education will save our race.

Following the devastating end of the war, Shimonaka's company began to reprint *The Great Encyclopedia*. Shortly thereafter, Heibonsha published *Shakaika Jiten* (*The Encyclopedia of Social Studies*), designed for the new course of social studies introduced during the American Occupation as a major democratic reform of the new school curriculum. He also published an encyclopedia for teachers on the same subject, in addition to a *Jidō Hyakka Jiten* (*Encyclopedia for Children*) in twenty-four volumes.

During the surge in publications by Heibonsha, Shimonaka himself was purged from public service by the American Occupation authorities for war crimes. He was forbidden from actively participating in the operation and management of his company until 1951. His son and his staff took over the company in order to carry out the founder's pledge to concentrate Heibonsha's publications in the field of education.

Once freed from the purge, Shimonaka regained his post as president of Heibonsha and launched into the publication of *The Great World Encyclopedia* in thirty-two volumes, which was finally completed in 1959. The publication represented the largest undertaking ever carried out by a publishing house in Japan. At the outset Shimonaka decided that the new encyclopedia would not concentrate on advanced western cultures, but would instead emphasize Asian cultures. The work also established

Heibonsha as the preeminent publisher of encyclopedias in Japan.

At the same time that Shimonaka plunged into this grand publishing venture upon being rehabilitated, he participated in various peace movements. During the autumn of 1951, he consulted with Kagawa Toyohiko, the famous Christian socialist, about establishing a new international organization called the World Federation of Nations to foster global unity following the devastating world war. As a result, the first international conference in Japan since the war, the Asian Conference for the World Federation of Nations, was held (appropriately) in Hiroshima the following year under the chairmanship of Shimonaka. Three hundred delegates from fourteen countries, including such distinguished guests as Malaysian Prime Minister Tuanku Abdul Rahman, signed the Hiroshima Declaration calling for a complete ban on the production and testing of nuclear weapons. The success of this initial meeting not only paved the way for a later Asian-African Conference in Bandung, Indonesia, but also contributed significantly to the development of an international movement against atomic bombs.

Shimonaka's underlying motivation for participating in these various movements derived from his conviction that World War II must end all wars on earth. At the ceremony marking the end of his rehabilitation, he argued that narrow nationalism should be replaced by international cooperation for a just and lasting peace. Since Japan had experienced the nuclear holocaust, the initiative against nuclear weapons should rightly come from the Japanese. Accordingly he devoted the rest of his life to carrying out the spirit of the new postwar constitution prohibiting war-making potential by Japan. His Committee of Seven, formed in 1955 and including Nobel laureate Yukawa Hideki, appealed to the United Nations to take more active measures for peace. His committee also appealed directly to the heads of state of the United States, the Soviet Union, and Great Britain to halt further testing of nuclear weapons.

At this time, Shimonaka the publisher promoted a new organization called the Publishers Association for Cultural Exchange. His first act was to visit China, which had suffered greatly during the war with Japan, as head of a delegation of Japanese publishers. An agreement was concluded that initiated the exchange of publications and technical developments in publishing between the two nations. It was also an attempt to promote reconciliation between two former bitter enemies.

Amid these many and varied activities aimed at building a new social order, Shimonaka suddenly died in 1961. His death brought to a close one of the most colorful and eventful careers in modern Japan. Shimonaka had burst upon the educational scene in prewar Japan as a defender of education for the masses. His famous May Day speech in 1920, which carried him into the limelight, called for equal opportunities for education for all, decrying the situation whereby the ignorant could enter the university if they could finance it.

Although indifferent to Marxist movements stirring at that time, Shimonaka's rhetoric and ideas appealed to many working-class people, upon whom he focused his attention. Indeed, his fame spread through his novel idea that teaching, traditionally considered a "holy profession," should be treated as an act of work; therefore, teachers are laborers no different from the general workforce. He scorned governmental policies that restricted teachers' social and political activities in the name of preserving their special status in society.

Shimonaka also looked upon education as a human right and one that should therefore be controlled by the people at the local level. This stance was in direct contradiction to Japanese tradition ever since the Meiji Restoration in 1868, at which time the central government set educational policy for the entire country in order to strengthen the nation as a whole. The result, according to Shimonaka, was evident in the standardization and uniformity of education, which stifled the individuality and creativity of the young. When the Fundamental Law of Education of 1947 called for local initiative in education, resulting in a locally elected lay school board system beginning in 1948, Shimonaka felt vindicated at last.

The final consideration of Shimonaka's long and varied career rightly concerns his inexplicable about-faces: from one of the most progressive thinkers in Japan, he became first a reactionary during the war, then an internationalist peace organizer after the war until the time of his death. He disastrously miscalculated

Japanese government intentions by failing to foresee the consequences of Japanese aggression cloaked in the false premise of expelling European colonizers from Asia. He was motivated by the attractive concept of Asia for the Asians.

Shimonaka was not alone among liberals in his circuitous path through modern Japanese history. Many other progressives underwent a similar wrenching experience under the extremely difficult conditions within Japanese society during the 1930s and 1940s. Still, the final decades of his life—devoted to movements promoting a peaceful world order devoid of nuclear weapons—reflected the ideas that originally carried Shimonaka into the very mainstream of Japanese education.

The Life of Shimonaka Yosaburo

1878	Born in Tatekui Village, Hyogo Prefecture.
1888	Attended local elementary school for three years; began working in the family tradition of pottery making.
1889	Became an assistant teacher at an elementary school in Kobe.
1902	Moved to Tokyo and began publishing a newspaper for children.
1904	Became a teacher at the Japan Women's School for Fine Arts.
1911	Joined the faculty of the Saitama Prefectural Normal School. Published *The Life of Saigo Takamori*.
1914	Established Heibonsha Publishing Company.
1919	Inaugurated Keimeikai (Enlightened Association) and began publishing *Keimei Journal*.
1920	Keimeikai renamed The Japanese Teachers' Union Enlightened Association.
1923	Published *Education for All Workers*; inaugurated the Century of Education Society.
1925	Inaugurated Farmers' Self-government Association.
1931	Began work on *The Great Encyclopedia*.
1940	Became committee chairman of an organization sup-

porting the Imperial Rule Assistance Association (Taisei Yokusankai).

1944 Published *My Thoughts*; joined the Supporters of the Imperial Land (Kokoku Dashikai) Association.

1946 Testified before the military occupation's tribunal investigating war crimes of the Japanese.

1948 Purged from public office for his wartime activities.

1951 Depurged and returned to Heibonsha; launched the movement for the World Federation of Nations.

1959 Published *The Great World Encyclopedia*.

1961 Died in Tokyo.

About the Author

Akira Nakano was born in 1929 in Aiichi Prefecture, and graduated from Tokyo Bunrika University in 1953. He has taught on the faculties of Kanazawa University, Wako University, and Rikkyo University, where he is now Professor. His publications (in Japanese) include *Liberal Education in the Taisho Period* (1967), *Educational Reformers* (1978), and *The Search for Life-long Education* (1981).

Nambara Shigeru in his later years.

Nambara Shigeru

[1889-1974]

Masao Terasaki

On February 11, 1946, barely six months after the upheavals of military defeat, a *kigensetsu* ceremony was staged at the large auditorium of Tokyo Imperial University (now the University of Tokyo). *Kigensetsu* was the traditional celebration of the national foundation day of Japan, commemorating the mythical accession of Emperor Jimmu in an ancient era. The scholar Nambara Shigeru, recently appointed as the first postwar head of this distinguished institution, addressed the gathering of students, faculty, and staff:

> The paramount challenge facing us today is none other than the cultivation of a new Japanese. To accomplish that we must deliberately create a revitalized spiritual movement. This is our only recourse to develop a new culture for Japan and to establish a moral nation founded on justice. Such a spiritual movement should permeate the entire country. The success or failure of the Showa Restoration depends on it. You students must assume responsibility by taking the lead. For this generation of young people searching for the truth, there is no greater challenge awaiting you.
>
> Either life or death; eternal humiliation or the recovery of freedom. We now stand at the crossroads. The choice is yours. The Potsdam Declaration that demanded our unconditional surrender did not result in our national extinction. The only path for us today is to contribute to the cultural and humanitarian progress of the world as a peace-loving nation among the new world order. My only fear

is that we may fail in this endeavor through our own idleness
and incompetence.

At this time, immediately after the war, the Japanese people
were suffering the terrible effects of severe food shortages, ram-
pant inflation, and social chaos. The Allied Occupation forces
had taken control of the country upon the collapse of the ultra-
militaristic Japanese regime. Under such circumstances the
spectacle of a ceremony commemorating the national foundation
day of Japan at the leading imperial university was viewed with
disbelief among the people. The national newspapers widely
reported the controversial event, quoting the president's words
calling for the Japanese people to literally rise up from military
defeat and contribute to the progress of the world. Intellectuals
and students compared President Nambara with Johann Fichte,
the great nineteenth-century German philosopher who aroused his
defeated nation, then under the military occupation of Napoleon's
army, with a speech. The historical parallel seemed fitting.

The new president of Tokyo Imperial University, in contrast
to his predecessors, had demonstrated an acute interest in the
prewar educational system. This carried over into the postwar
years when he passionately advocated a spiritual revolution as
the foundation for the reconstruction of Japanese education. A
spiritual awakening was to him the essence of a new democratic
Japan. Accordingly, he assumed the role in postwar Japan not
of a classroom teacher but of an "educator of the public." His
eloquent address to the students and faculty of the nation's leading university in early 1946 marked his emergence as one of the
greatest educators Japan has ever produced.

Nambara Shigeru was born in an obscure village in Kagawa
Prefecture, northern Shikoku, in 1889, under the family name
of Minamibara. Later, during his high-school days in Tokyo,
many of his friends called him Nambara, since the Chinese character for "south" in his name can be pronounced either "minami"
or "nan(m)." He used the "Nambara" pronounciation from that
time onward.

The Nambara family experienced hardships and trials from
the very beginning in the tiny village, with the mother exhibiting

A group portrait with fellow students at the First National Higher School, around 1909. Nambara is second from the left in the back row.

In Berlin, 1923.

Nambara as a young father in 1929.

Departing for the United States, 1949.

industriousness while the father was indulgent. They divorced when their son was only two years old. He was brought up by his mother and her family while she eked out a living teaching sewing to neighborhood girls. It was not a propitious childhood for the future president of the University of Tokyo.

Shigeru proved to be a brillant lad, entering school at the age of five rather than the usual six, the rules being relaxed because of the boy's demonstrated ability. In the early 1900s, few children advanced beyond the first elementary school section of four years, the vast majority dropping out to look for some type of simple work. It was precisely at this time, 1901, that a prefectural teacher training institute was established in Shikoku designed to produce "junior teachers" for primary schools to meet the needs of the rapidly expanding elementary school population. Nambara, upon completion of the four-year elementary course, entered the new institute to study pedagogy, teaching methods, and psychology for precisely one year. He received a junior teacher's license in 1902, at the tender age of twelve. Such was the state of Japanese education at the turn of the century.

Following the year spent at the Institute, the young teenager promptly advanced to the local middle school, a branch of the Prefectural Takamatsu Secondary School. During the five-year course, Nambara consistently ranked at the head of his class. Based on his outstanding academic record, he was able to sit for and pass the formidable entrance examination to enter the most prestigious secondary school in the nation, the First National Higher School in Tokyo. Graduates of this institution customarily entered Tokyo Imperial University.

The progression of Nambara's education from a rural elementary school to the elite preparatory school in Tokyo is of great historical relevance to the understanding of his thought and role in postwar Japanese education. His native village of Aioi, located on the shores of Shikoku in far-off Kagawa Prefecture, supported no industry. Consequently the local people worked partly in agriculture on tiny farms in the region's mild climate, and partly at fishing in the Inland Sea. Village life was desperately poor, including that of the Nambara family. Near the village is a historic area called Yashima where, during the twelfth century, the Genji clan was defeated by the Heike clan to lose control of the sea lanes. The area was therefore of some historical interest.

In later life Nambara often referred to his beloved birthplace and his hard-working mother in *tanka* poetry inspired by many visits to his native village. One of his poems was inscribed on a monument erected in 1958 in his memory on the Osaka ridge where he had often hiked as a child. A loose translation reflects his feelings:

> On the Osaka ridge
> Where I often hiked in my childhood
> Here I stand in awe
> Looking down upon my beloved birthplace.

Later in life, Nambara often used such terms in his writings as "homeland" (*sokoku*) and "the community of man" (*minzoku kyo-dotai*).These expressions were not those of a nationalist but rather the expression of a reverent affection toward traditional culture. This attitude motivated him to hold the famous National Foundation Day ceremony in 1946, within six months of Japan's military and economic collapse.

Another factor in Nambara's youth that underlay his contribution to Japanese education in both the pre- and postwar eras was his mother's abiding interest in education. She regarded teaching as an ideal vocation for the son who exhibited such a keen mind as a child. It was through her convictions that her son entered the new teacher training institute located near the family village, even though he was only eleven years old. A letter written at the age of nine, discovered in archives, expresses not only the young boy's hopes for his future, but also his mother's desires: "I hope to go on to the higher elementary school course. Then I want to go to another country to study more. That way I can help to improve the way of education, and my country as well."

In the context of the time and place, "another country" meant to the people in this local village a large city far from home, such as Tokyo. Indeed, one of Nambara's teachers repeatedly told him that he should go to Tokyo to study when he grew up. His other reference, to improving "the way of education," was evidence of an idealism in this young boy that set him apart from his contemporaries. In retrospect, we can see that at the age of nine Nambara had already chosen his priorities for life, which ultimately came to fruition when he emerged as one of the leading reformers of postwar Japanese education. Among the presidents of the University of Tokyo, Nambara stands out as the one most interested in Japanese education, with the roots of that interest embedded in his mother's expectations and his short but highly influential course at the teacher training institute.

Entry into the liberal arts course of the First National Higher School marked the monumental transition from local education to the elite national course for outstanding students. It brought Nambara under the influence of another of Japan's great educators, the kind and gentle Nitobe Inazo, the school's principal. His years at the First National Higher School were the very time when bright young men were seeking their own identities and aims in life amid the political and social confusion stemming from the Russo-Japanese War of 1904–5. Although the liberal arts course traditionally led to Tokyo or Kyoto Imperial Universities, followed by upper-echelon government service, Nambara experienced an identity crisis whose nature he revealed in a later speech at his old middle school:

> Coming under the tutelage of Principal Nitobe was a wonderfully provocative experience for us. We formed small reading circles and discussed passionately the meaning of life and truth. We wrestled with our development as humanists. For us, learning from textbooks was of secondary importance. The most important concern was to cultivate ourselves as human beings.

Nevertheless the young Nambara experienced internal struggles and worries. He reflected in another speech that the more he struggled with the meaning of life, the larger loomed the problems he faced. This identification problem was shared by many of his fellow students who had been carefully screened from local communities and suddenly thrust into the nation's elite preparatory school. The abrupt transition from local feudal customs to the rapidly modernizing capital city of Tokyo had an incalculable impact on the boys. On top of that dislocation, the school curriculum introduced these bright local students to modern science and humanities based on western concepts incompatible with Japanese traditions and customs. Although the teenaged Nambara was not alone in confronting a strange new world, he was one of the most serious in searching for answers to the complexities of life.

The principal of the First National Higher School in Nambara's day, Nitobe Inazo, was a pillar of the Christian movement in Japan, along with his friend Uchimura Kanzo, another of Japan's great educators. A number of students at this famous preparatory school came under the lasting influence of Uchimura through his private Bible classes, which were recommended by Nitobe. In 1911, at the age of twenty-one, Nambara joined Uchimura's private study group; impressed with readings from the journal *Seisho no Kenkyu* (*Bible Study*), edited by the teacher, he became a convert to Christianity.

The volatile and provocative Uchimura was at that time launching his great non-church Christian movement in Japan. Coincidentally, Nambara was searching for a purpose in life. Uchimura's teachings denied the deeply imbedded Confucian morality that Nambara had learned during his rural childhood. A leading student of Uchimura and a contemporary of Nambara, the political scientist Fukuda Kin'ichi, divided into three areas the beliefs held by Nambara which were directly influenced by Uchimura: (1) base everything on the simple foundation of historical Christianity; (2) confront the Imperial regime, especially the ideology of the *kokutai*, the Imperial state; and (3) cultivate a national identity through universal truths and the realization of a national mission based on them. A fourth might have been included— the awakening of the basic intelligence and inherent spirit to realize that national mission. These fundamental concepts ran consistently through Nambara's thought and actions during the monumental postwar reforms of Japanese education.

In 1910 Nambara entered the highly prestigious Faculty of Law of Tokyo Imperial University. At that time the Faculty of Law was divided into two academic disciplines, law and political science. Although the law course held the paramount position in the Faculty, Nambara chose political science, apparently because of his inclination toward philosophical and theoretical studies.

Early on Nambara came under the influence of Professor Kakei Katsuhiko, a distinguished scholar who taught courses on Japanese law, jurisprudence, and public administration. He was also well known for teaching the philosophy of law from a Buddhist perspective, later becoming a nationalist scholar with a Shinto perspective. Kakei was well aware of Nambara's different background as a Christian interested in German idealism. Nevertheless the two developed a warm personal student-teacher relationship.

Nambara proved to be a highly diligent student. Mano Tsuyoshi, who became a Justice of the Supreme Court after the war, fondly remembered his former classmate as extraordinarily devoted to his studies. Another postwar justice, Kobayashi Shunzo, described his fellow student in the Faculty of Law as a model student. He compared Nambara's daily routine of study, class attendance, and library research to the punctual operation of the Japan National Railways.

Nambara's life as a student in the Faculty of Law at Japan's most prominent university in the early 1900s was, however, not that different from that of his classmates. There were nearly two thousand students enrolled in the Faculty of Law, representing about half the total student population of the university. Their future careers depended to a great extent on their course grades. The competition to enter government bureaus, especially the Ministries of Home Affairs and Finance, motivated the students to study diligently.

In his attention to his studies Nambara was not dramatically different from his classmates, who devoted many hours each day to memorizing the contents of lectures and reading assignments for examinations that demanded a broad knowledge of facts and information. What set him apart from many of them was his interest in the philosophical background of modern theories of government which were rooted in the writings of the great philosophers of the past. His distinctive interest in broad philosophical concerns during his university years was a clear indication that Nambara was destined for a career well beyond the life of a Japanese bureaucrat, no matter how attractive that was to most graduates.

In 1914 Nambara graduated. He was one of five outstanding graduates of the Faculty of Law who were awarded silver watches by the Emperor. Along with a number of his fellow classmates from the Faculty, Nambara immediately entered the Ministry of Home Affairs. He had become convinced that he could best serve society not through a posting at ministry headquarters in Tokyo, but by serving in a rural area working with the local people. Accordingly he was assigned as a supervisor of a rural district in Toyama Prefecture, where he became involved in local affairs while also devoting his energies to the establishment of a public agricultural training school. He wrote at that time that in order to understand the politics of a nation, it was essential to live among the people in the countryside.

He was reassigned to the ministerial headquarters two years later, just as the activities of the Japanese labor movement reached a peak. Nambara was given the task of drafting the provisions of regulations governing the organization of labor unions. The proposal was intended for Cabinet approval, but it was subsequently shelved when the Agriculture and Commerce Ministries opposed it as overly restrictive to management.

This action proved to be the turning point in Nambara's life. In 1921, at the age of thirty-two, he resigned from the Ministry to accept an appointment as Associate Professor in the Faculty of Law of Tokyo Imperial University. He was immediately sent to Europe to begin a three-year study program that included periods at the Universities of Berlin, London, and Grenoble. It was not unusual for a newly appointed faculty member of Japan's leading university to be sent abroad for study before assuming a teaching position. However, in Nambara's case, he had a definite purpose and even a specific subject to research. He revealed his motives in a later speech:

> I had come to the conclusion that the social unrest and labor demands troubling Japan at the time were the result of Marxist influence. I decided that the only way to tackle the problem in Japan was to go to the very source of that influence. I turned in my resignation to the Ministry and

was fortunate to receive an appointment at the university which enabled me to go to Germany where Marx himself was born and educated. I immediately undertook the study of the same German philosophers that Marx had studied. However, I followed the reverse study course of Marx, that is, from Hegel to Fichte to Kant.

Although the conclusions he reached as a result of this period abroad were not published for twenty years after his return to Japan, the philosophical foundations of Nambara as a political scientist were formed in Europe. He declared himself henceforth an anti-Marxist liberal. During the war, he wrote that he regarded both Marxism and modern positivism as evidence of the crisis of modern culture. Throughout his life, he was deeply opposed to Marxism. In this sense, Nambara, along with many of the university professors in the humanities and social sciences who were expelled from their positions during the war, can be recognized as true liberals.

The twenty years that Nambara served on the faculty of Tokyo Imperial University were marked by a slow but continual advancement within the academic discipline of political science. Initially he was in charge of the required general courses of the Department of Law. In 1929 he assumed the professorial chair in political science and responsibility for the specialist courses taught by his former teacher, Onozuka Kiheji, the founder of modern political science in Japan, who was appointed president of the university in 1929.

The so-called chair system had been introduced from European universities into Japan's imperial universities in 1892. Holding the top chair in any department as the professor in that department's discipline gave the holder recognition as one of the most authoritative scholars in the field. To hold the professorial position at Tokyo Imperial University was to be virtually preeminent in one's field in Japan.

Since Nambara served as Professor of Political Science at Japan's leading university from 1930 to the 1940s, he was regarded as the foremost authority in the field for a decade and a half. His tenure was noted primarily for two developments of the time. The first was his passion in defense of academic freedom of the university during the wartime period when the Japanese government was controlled by the military. The other was his profound influence on his students, many of whom were to become political leaders after the war during the great democratization period.

The long period when Nambara served on the faculty of Tokyo Imperial University coincides with the rise of fascism in Europe and ultranationalism and militarism in Japan. During this monumental era in modern world history, all Japanese universities underwent the wrenching suppression of academic freedom by the military authorities then in control of the government, who focused especially on the social science and humanities faculties. Such infamous incidents took place as the right-wing attack on Professor Minobe Tatsukichi for his critical interpretation of the Imperial Constitution and his theory that the Emperor was an organ of the state, and the arrests of Professors Ouchi Hyoe and Arisawa Hiromi for their political activities. In 1938, the Minister of Education, General Sadao Araki, attempted to deprive the faculty of the right to select new appointments and to elect university presidents.

During these difficult years, when Japan was inexorably sliding into full-scale war, the militarists and the ultra-conservatives conspired to suppress both Marxist and non-Marxist liberals on university faculties. They targeted those within the departments of law and economics because of their opposition to the revered concept of *kokutai*—a national polity centered around the Emperor which was heralded by ultranationalists as the driving force of Japan as the center of a new Asia devoid of western influence.

Nambara resolutely defended the principal of academic freedom of the university. In 1938, he publicly opposed the Ministry of Education's efforts to usurp the power of new appointments and the selection of the university president. He argued that the Japanese university has the authority to manage its own faculty appointments and select its administrative officers. He compared the reforms proposed by the Minister of Education, General Araki, to those being carried out by the Nazis in Germany. They should, Nambara declared, not be implemented at Japanese universities.

During this critical period Nambara defended the principle of academic freedom in various writings including *University Autonomy* [*Daigaku no Jichi*] (1938), *The Foundations of the University* [*Daigaku no Honshitsu*] (1941), *The State and Learning* [*Kokka to Gakumon*] (1942), and *War and Culture* [*Senso to Bunka*] (1944). He held the strong conviction that a university should be managed by its faculty. Throughout the war, whenever the university president or outside forces attempted to infringe on faculty autonomy, the Law Faculty under Nambara strongly criticized such action.

His tanka poetry, published in a collection after the war, revealed Nambara's anguish at events taking place within the university during wartime. A dismissal of a colleague from the Economics Faculty without faculty consent inspired this poem while Nambara served as a member of the University Council:

> With renewed courage
> I said what I should.
> I may never meet him again.

During the same period, Nambara invited the distinguished scholar Tsuda Sokichi to join his Faculty of Law. Tsuda, then a professor at the private Waseda University, had become a controversial figure as a result of a governmental ban on the publication of several of his books, including critical analyses of the ancient anthologies *Kojiki* and *Nihonshoki*. These two works contained the mythical stories of ancient Japan upon which the ultraconservatives based their beliefs and teachings in the supernatural origins of the original Imperial Family. Nambara respected Tsuda's academic work and devoted his energies to shielding the scholar from the inevitable attacks by right-wing radicals.

During his years at the university, Nambara pursued the life of a scholar by reading books, preparing lectures, and giving examinations. Some of his students and friends affectionately dubbed him the "philosopher in a cave." Nevertheless his lectures during this tense period of military domination and Japanese expansion attracted many eager students.

One of his illustrious students, Igarashi Toyosaka, who took Nambara's classes in politics and the history of politics, described his courses as both speculative and logical. He felt that the lectures attracted many students because they were based on philosophy as well as politics. Indeed, the lectures began with the basic question, What is politics? In other words, it was political philosophy based on a new idealism that Nambara was teaching, evolving from his conviction that neither existing politics nor empirical science provided the answers to his fundamental question.

Nambara's reputation attracted many bright students who were to become outstanding proponents of the new democracy after the war. Among them were such scholars as Oka Yoshitake, Nakamura Akira, Maruyama Masao, Ogata Norio, Tsuji Kiyoaki, Fukuda Kanichi, and Saito Makoto, to name but a few of those who distinguished themselves as the new era in Japanese postwar history unfolded. They revealed how deeply their former teacher influenced their lives in a collection of affectionate memories published in 1975.

One of the most important of Nambara's publications was his treatise *The State and Religion* [*Kokka to Shukyo*], published in 1943, at the very peak of World War II. The subtitle, "A Study of the Spiritual History of Europe," indicates that it was an outgrowth of his studies in Europe more than twenty years earlier. It represented a rather unique analysis of the political history of Europe through the spiritual or religious developments in the relationship between politics and religion. The coverage runs from Plato through Kant and Hegel to the Nazi era.

The final chapter in this book, "Religion From the Nazi Perspective," deserves attention not only because of its content. The fact that it was published at a time when the Japanese military government had concluded an alliance with Nazi Germany is remarkable in itself. It marked Nambara as a radical in the academic world who opposed Japanese fascism. He summarized Nazi ideology in this way:

> I concluded that Nazi ideology attempted to integrate ancient Greek culture with Christianity. It was finally compelled to deny Christianity in an endeavor to base itself on northern European traditions, those of Germany, thus alienating itself from traditional European culture imbedded in

Christianity. It stems from the powerful nihilism of Nietsche, and is consequently essentially counter to the traditional positivism of European Christian culture. If the Nazis intend to spread their ideology over Europe, they will inevitably fail. If they want to establish a new European order, they must revise their ideology to succeed. Nazism, born in crisis, is no less than a total negation of the European spirit, the classical Greek philosophy of searching for truth for truth's sake, and the universality of Christianity. It cannot prevail.

Nambara not only risked his academic position by writing theses counter to the propaganda of the Japanese military government then at total war with European and North American countries; he risked his life at the same time. In early 1945, under the most adverse of circumstances, he initiated a movement for peace within the ranks of sympathetic faculty members of his university. Although the war was suddenly brought to an end, with the unexpected nuclear bombing of Hiroshima and Nagasaki, before the movement had a chance to develop, it set the stage for Nambara's role in the postwar democratization of Japanese society.

In December 1945, Nambara's colleagues elected him President of Tokyo Imperial University, which was soon to be renamed the University of Tokyo. At the time, he was serving as Dean of the Faculty of Law, a position that often served as a stepping-stone to the presidency. However, he was specifically chosen by the faculty members to reform and reconstruct the university following the severe trauma of the war and military domination of the country.

Shortly before the election, the *University Gazette*, in its first postwar issue, contained a lengthy article written by Nambara. It was entitled "The Postwar Mission of the University: To the Demobilized Students." He wrote that with the end of the war and the occupation of Japan by a victorious foreign army, no one could foretell what demands would be made of the Japanese people. Under these circumstances, how could Japan reconstruct itself? The answer, he said, can be found only in education. In a defeated nation with few natural resources, the university, as the highest institution of learning, assumes a unique role. Although education from the elementary school through the university must be completely reformed based on humanism, the university must take the lead. Nambara was elected to carry out his own mandate.

Two major challenges faced the new president. The immediate concern involved a reorganization of the university in accordance with the new regulations governing higher education to be drawn up under the American Occupation authorities—better known as SCAP, for the Supreme Commander of the Allied Powers, General Douglas MacArthur. The second was to maintain the autonomy of the university even though the country and its Ministry of Education were in fact under the complete control of a foreign military government.

But Nambara was quickly drawn into matters extending far beyond the reorganization of his own university. He was to play a leading role in the reform of Japanese education from top to bottom. There are knowledgeable Japanese who are convinced that the postwar democratization of Japanese education would not have been carried out nearly as effectively had it not been for the pivotal role that Nambara played. That unique role began virtually from the very beginning of the Occupation, in 1945–46, and continued to its ending in 1952.

The instrument which enabled Nambara to exert such an enormous influence on the direction of educational reform in postwar Japan was his position on the Council on Educational Reform (Kyoiku Sasshin Shingikai). He served initially as vice-chairman, from August 1946 to October 1947, and then as chairman until the end of the Occupation. Although reluctant at first to accept a major responsibility outside his university post, Nambara finally agreed to the committee assignment upon realizing the potential for change that the Council represented. It functioned as an advisory committee under the Prime Minister's Office, established to work with SCAP's educational reformers; its fifty-odd members represented a cross-section of the society. Through its twenty-one committees, it deliberated on the new laws governing education, including the Fundamental Law of Education, the School Education Act, the School Board Law, the Special Law Governing Teachers and Teaching Licenses, and the Law for Social Education. In all these areas the

Council under Nambara exerted a strong influence on the proposals that ultimately became law.

But even before the Council was formed, Nambara had independently established within his university a study committee for the reform of Japanese education. Consisting of distinguished scholars from each faculty, the committee, which was formed in January 1946, discussed not only the reform of the university system but a reform plan for the entire national system of education. It is assumed that the committee members were well aware of the impending visit of the first United States Education Mission to Japan. Nambara apparently wanted to be prepared to tell the U.S. Mission members the views of the professors from Japan's leading university.

The ad-hoc committee submitted a reform plan to President Nambara calling for five years of elementary schooling, a three-year middle school, and a four-year high school, to be followed by a four-year university course. It also recommended simplifying the highly complicated school structure. One of the most famous members, Kaigo Muneomi, an associate professor of pedagogy, chaired the committee that drew up the reform plans. When the U.S. Mission arrived in Japan in March 1946, Nambara was prepared with Kaigo's report from the Japanese side.

On March 21, Nambara met with George D. Stoddard, head of the Mission, and outlined his ideas for reform based on the committee's recommendations. Several days later, Takagi Yasaka, a member of the Law Faculty of the University of Tokyo, called on Robert King Hall of the Civil Information and Education Department of SCAP to make a similar report. The primary difference between the two was Nambara's concern for the importance of moral and spiritual instruction in the new system of education.

At these meetings with the American officials, both Nambara and Takagi pointed out the defects of Japanese education. They contended that: (1) it does not provide sufficient educational opportunities for the masses; (2) the system is far too complex with a variety of schools at each level; (3) the system favors certain privileged sectors in the society; (4) women have virtually no opportunity for university education; and (5) normal schools produce teachers with a narrow specialized training.

The reform proposals submitted by Nambara to overcome these defects called for a revision of Japanese education along the lines of the American model, in a step-by-step sequence with each school level moving the students in a natural progression up the ladder of education to the next level. This was in sharp contrast to the wide diversity of schools in Japan, which were mostly unrelated to each other above the elementary level. Emphasizing equality of educational opportunity, the plan incorporated the specialized higher schools into a broad university system.

The Japanese proposal finally submitted by Nambara and Takagi to the American authorities advocated an educational structure that was designed to reach the masses, enlighten them through education about their rights, and instill in the general populace democratic ideas; to incorporate a six-year elementary school and a three-year middle school common to all students, followed by a three-year high school; to eliminate the prestigious boys' high school (*koto gakko*) as the source of educational distortions favoring a few select males, along with other specialized secondary schools; to provide a graded system of integrated schools all of which led either to a terminal course or to higher education; to eliminate the differences between specialized higher schools (including those for teacher training) and universities by incorporating all institutions at the higher level into a unified comprehensive university system; and to abolish the division between boys' schools and girls' schools, and establish coeducation throughout.

A comparison of the educational reforms ultimately carried out under SCAP edict and the reform proposals recommended by Nambara shows a remarkable similarity. Nambara and his colleagues exhibited foresight few would have believed possible in a nation in ruin after military defeat.

According to recent Japanese research into this era, shortly after Nambara met with leaders of the United States Education Mission, which drew up the general plan in just one month's visit for the educational reforms implemented later, the following insertion was made in their report:

It is further proposed that the first six years be spent in

primary schools as at present, and the next three years in a "lower secondary school" to be developed through merging and modifying the many kinds of schools which those completing primary school now enter. . . . It is proposed further that a three-year "upper secondary school" be established, free of tuition costs, in time to be co-educational, and providing varied opportunities for all who wish to continue their education.

Many years later Nambara was asked whether the 6–3–3 system, a fundamental revision of the Japanese school structure carried out during the Occupation, was in fact included in his committee's report as a result of American influence, since it resembled the American system. He strongly denied this, claiming that the proposal originated among the Japanese members themselves. Recent scholarship supports Nambara's contention.

One of the other major reforms promoted by Nambara was the abolishment of the old normal school system, of which he had become critical as far back as the 1920s. In the deliberations of his Council on Educational Reform after the war, he argued against it pursuasively. He explained his position at a later date:

> One of the most important problems we faced at that time was the reform of teacher education. I thought it was critical that we educate a new teacher who could contribute to the development of a new Japan. I could not accept the situation in which graduates of specialized schools (*senmon gakko*) were responsible for the nation's compulsory education. Graduates of universities should assume that heavy responsibility. That was why so many new universities were established after the war.

It must be remembered that during his chairmanship of the Council on Educational Reform, he continued to hold the position of President of the University of Tokyo. At that time the discipline of education or teacher training was not part of the curriculum. Nambara took the lead in establishing a new Faculty of Education at this most influential institution of higher education in the land. It was a bold and difficult move on the part of the president of a university which up to then did not recognize education as a discipline for academic study.

Officials at SCAP, notably W. C. Eels and V. A. Curley, had emphasized the need for a faculty of education at the former imperial universities. Nambara supported that proposal from SCAP because it reflected his personal view on the issue and that expressed by the Council on Educational Reform. Even though his own personal experience at a prewar teacher training institution as a lad of eleven was a positive one, he was convinced that educational reform for a new democratic Japan required the elimination of normal schools.

The other important reform of the University of Tokyo under President Nambara was the establishment of a new Faculty of Liberal Arts. The old imperial universities were noted for their specialized studies on the European model. To many scholars, the more specialized a department was, the more academically prestigious it became. Nambara took the lead in this controversy when he argued that the prewar upper secondary schools (*koto gakko*) were essentially appendages of higher education, instruments providing a type of liberal education for an elite class similar to eighteenth-century British "gentlemen." The privileged students coming out of the thirty-three preparatory schools into the seven imperial universities formed a unified system that was difficult to change since many faculty members felt a strong loyalty toward these schools.

The postwar reforms of education were aimed at developing good citizens, according to Nambara. The higher secondary schools were being abolished. Consequently, Nambara argued, the university must incorporate in its new structure a liberal arts program to provide a broad general education program for the new leaders of Japan before they begin their specialized studies. As a result the University of Tokyo established the first and only Faculty of Liberal Arts within the national university system.

Among the other changes brought about under President Nambara was the construction of dormitories for students suffering from the shortages of all goods after the war. He also supported the establishment of the first western-style university press in Japan, the University of Tokyo Press, and served as chairman of its first Board of Directors.

To Nambara, the object of all these reforms was the establishment of a new university system with a broad clientele, which would serve as a cornerstone of the postwar mass system of education. The prewar elite upper secondary schools (*koto gakko*) and the rigid teacher training schools (*shihan gakko*) had been special targets of his criticism for many years. Having opposed their existence before the war, Nambara at last witnessed their demise in the postwar era.

Underlying Nambara's opposition to SCAP's plans for the reformation of university administration and his efforts promoting the new Fundamental Law of Education is his profound interest in university autonomy and freedom of education. Those concerns grew out of his bitter experiences under prewar governmental oppression and his vision of an egalitarian education in postwar democratic Japan. His ultimate feelings were expressed in a speech at a National Association of Education conference held in Washington in 1949 to consider education in American-occupied nations:

> The most formidable problem we face today is the formulation of the principles of education in contemporary Japan and the spiritual foundation underlying them. The aim of education must be the development of individuality founded on the freedom of learning. This formed the basis of the western Renaissance many years ago. Japan must experience her own Renaissance today.
>
> The Meiji Restoration of 1868 ushered in the so-called modern era of Japanese history. It offered an unprecedented opportunity for a fundamental reformation of Japanese society, a Japanese Renaissance as it were. Rather, the leaders committed the cardinal sin of establishing priorities aimed at expanding the nation's power and wealth. Values pertaining to individuality were subordinated to the interests of the state. But it is never too late to correct the course of history. Now is the time to carry out a Japanese Renaissance through the reform of education and the redemption of universal humanism.

Nambara's concept of educational reform embodied not only

the reform of educational practices but also a total renaissance of mankind. The new postwar Constitution that replaced the prewar Meiji Imperial Constitution, along with the Fundamental Law of Education that supplanted the prewar Imperial Rescript, were all symbolic of the coming Renaissance. The very essence of the new era was evidenced in the statutory provisions incorporated in the revolutionary clause "educational opportunity for all." To Nambara, the military defeat of Japan had been transformed into a blessing in disguise, leading to a spiritual revolution of the Japanese people through education. Nambara took solace in having played a leading role in constructing the foundation.

In March 1974, nearly three decades after the war, Nambara Shigeru died at the venerable age of eighty-five. Seventeen years earlier, following an address at his own elementary school in Kagawa, where he often returned bringing gifts of his calligraphy that are treasured there to this day, he had been stricken with a heart attack. His physical condition forced him to sharply curtail his activities, convalescing for a short period in the town where he was brought up.

Partially recovered by the age of eighty-two, Nambara wrote his last book, *Introduction to Political Philosophy* [*Seiji Tetsugaku Josetsu*], while serving as Director of the Japan Academy. His last few years were spent quietly, in contrast to his long and active career spanning both the pre- and postwar eras; in both he was known as one of Japan's greatest educators.

The Life of Nambara Shigeru

1889   Born in Aioi Village, Kagawa Prefecture.
1901   Entered Okawa Teachers' Training Institute.
1902   Passed the examination as a junior teacher in the elementary school.
1907   Entered First National Higher School.
1910   Entered Tokyo Imperial University, where he studied politics.

1911   Converted to Christianity.
1914   Entered the Ministry of Home Affairs.
1921   Appointed Associate Professor at Tokyo Imperial University.
1925   Named Professor in the Faculty of Law.
1942   Published *Kokka to Shukyo* [*The State and Religion*].
1945   Elected President, Tokyo Imperial University (renamed University of Tokyo in 1946).
1946   Named Chairman of the Japanese Committee to Cooperate with the U.S. Education Mission.
1947   Appointed Chairman of the Kyoiku Sasshin Iinkai (Council on Educational Reform); established the National Association of University Professors.
1957   Named emeritus professor, University of Tokyo.
1964   Elected Director of the Japan Academy; published *Nihon no Riso* [*Ideals of Japan*].
1969   Published *Rekishi o Tsukuru Mono* [*Creators of History*].
1974   Died at the age of 85.

About the Author

Masao Terasaki was born in 1932 in Fukuoka Prefecture. He received the Doctor of Education degree in 1964 from the University of Tokyo, where he is currently Professor in the Faculty of Education. His publications (in Japanese) include *The Development of University Self-Government in Japan* (1979) and (as co-author) *University Education* (1969).

Munakata Seiya in 1969.

Munakata Seiya

[1908–1970]

Muneaki Mochizuki

On June 24, 1970, two days after his death, a memorial service
was held by the Japan Teachers' Union in honor of Munakata
Seiya. Many messages of condolence were given on that occasion.
Among them, two stand out as important for the analysis of
Munakata's contribution to Japanese education.

Professor Kaigo Muneomi of the University of Tokyo recognized Munakata's instrumental efforts in forming the Japan
Society for the Study of Education after the war. During the
twenty-year period of its existence, Munakata made a major
contribution to the Society's growth and development. He served
as a director of this most important independent educational
organization for most of its existence.

According to Professor Kaigo, Munakata was a specialist in
educational administration. He was especially interested in the
role of the central government in local educational administration in a democratic system of education. His views on this problem were influential in determining the character and policy of
the Japan Society for the Study of Education.

When the Society established a special committee on educational administration in 1954, Munakata was appointed its first
chairman and directed its varied activities for many years. From
1961 through 1966 he served as Chairman of the Study Committee
on the Fundamental Law of Education, in which capacity he
actively led the movement to preserve the law itself and to
promote its aims. Also, as a member of the Science Council of
Japan from 1959, Munakata directed his efforts in maintaining

close relations between the Council and the Japan Society for the Study of Education.

Shortly after World War II, Professor Kaigo, one of the most distinguished scholars at the University of Tokyo, was instrumental in drawing up a plan for a new College of Education within the University. Included in the initial scheme was a Department of Educational Administration to study the relationship between the state and the school. At that time this was an entirely new field of academic study. Consequently it was decided to appoint a young and energetic scholar to head the department. Munakata, then on the faculty of Tokyo Bunri University, was appointed the first Professor of Educational Administration at the University of Tokyo.

As the first scholar to hold the chair in educational administration at the most prestigious university in the land, Munakata broke new ground through the scientific approach to the study of educational administration. From the time of his appointment to his retirement from the University, he devoted all of his efforts to the development of this new discipline. Not only was he a distinguished scholar in the world of academics; he followed the day-to-day problems of the school as it was influenced by the educational policies of the government. He developed a sharp and critical attitude toward the national policy for education, for which he became well known throughout Japan.

The President of the Japan Teachers' Union, Makieda Motofumi, paid his deepest respects at the funeral for Munakata's support for and involvement in the teachers' organized movement in the postwar era. According to Makieda:

> Munakata immediately after the war devoted himself to the study of education for the primary purpose of building a democratic school system for a new democratic society. With the shift in governmental policy in the 1950s from a democratic basis to a nationalistic one, Munakata joined with 600,000 members of the Japan Teachers' Union to fight against the increasing power of the state.
>
> The relationship between Professor Munakata and the Japan Teachers' Union began in 1951, when he agreed to serve on a special committee to draft a code of ethics for

Munakata as a primary-school
student in Miyagi Prefecture, ca.
1919.

Teachers survey the site of a new building for Seikatsu Gakuen, which was
destroyed during World War II. Munakata is second from the right. 1945.

The Munakata family in Mejiro, Tokyo, ca. 1948.

In the 1950s, at an early Conference for the Study of Education, sponsored by the Japan Teachers' Union.

teachers, which declared that "teachers are laborers." Then, with the outbreak of the Korean War, Professor Munakata supported and encouraged the union's movement against rearmament under the slogan "Never send our children into battle again." The members looked upon this campaign as a mission of the union.

In the autumn of the same year, the union held its first National Teachers' Conference for the Study of Education. The union had been struggling to overcome the effects of the severe postwar depression, in which teachers worked for pitifully low wages. Under the most trying conditions of the time, it was extremely difficult to organize a national teachers' meeting to consider the problems of the school. Nevertheless, Professor Munakata, facing the challenge of his new academic post at the University of Tokyo, worked closely with the union to stage this historical study conference of teachers, the first of its kind since the war.

The initial conference proved to be a difficult one in which inexperience and lack of orientation led to considerable confusion and disorder. On the final day, having observed the meeting from beginning to end, Professor Munakata spoke to the delegates accordingly: "Perhaps your enthusiasm for teaching provoked the many emotional disputes and controversies that we witnessed this week. However, your mission is to build a new educational system for the people of Japan on the foundation of peace and democracy. In this grand endeavor, you should not lose your self-control. You must rationally study the problems of education in their social, economical, and political context." From that moment onward for the next twenty years, Professor Munakata played an extremely active role in the organized teachers' movement in Japan.

In the union's reaction against what was viewed as the oppressive actions of the government toward the teachers' movement, Chairman Makieda confessed:

We sometimes acted impetuously. On those occasions Professor Munakata admonished us to act prudently and creatively in developing a spirit of resistance within the framework of the Constitution and the Fundamental Law of Education. Following his convictions as a scholar of school administration, he criticized the reactionary policies of the government that were implemented through the Law for the Maintenance of Political Neutrality of Education and the Law for the Organization and Management of Local Educational Administration. His support and encouragement gave life to our struggle against these critical ordinances.

When the government enforced the Teachers' Efficiency Rating scheme and the National Scholastic Achievement Tests, Professor Munakata spoke out forcefully against these devices aimed at weakening our power. In the struggle, some of our teachers were arrested for opposing those policies. He stood at the courts of justice and eloquently defended our colleagues and condemned their arrests as an unjust act of the government in its attempt to usurp educational control. Ironically, the Supreme Court recently acquitted several defendants who were brought to trial in an incident over the use of the Teachers' Efficiency Rating System in Tokyo. Without Professor Munakata's assistacce, we could not have won this case, which shows how this distinguished scholar on education was also a man who became actively involved in the struggle to preserve democracy in education.

We can see through the memorial addresses of these two leading figures in the Japanese world of education how Munakata played a leading role in the postwar developments of Japanese education. It is thus rather difficult to imagine that he was in essence a prewar man, having been born in Tokyo in the year 1908. His father, a principal of a local secondary school, had a great influence on his life. He once wrote of his father that he was truly a Meiji man, having been born one year before the Meiji Restoration, in 1867, and died just as the Pacific War broke out. He was remembered as a man of firm character, typical of the image of a Meiji man. A note in his diary from his days as a school principal was included in an essay written by Munakata, indicating the kind of memories of his father that he carried with him through life:

"It was learned that one of our male students exchanged love
letters with a girl from a nearby girls' school. Today I interviewed him and, upon orders from the local school authorities, expelled him from the school. He is an excellent
student whose passion led him astray. I feel as if my heart
is breaking."

Munakata concluded that although his father was "a man of
strong character, he did not take action without pity. It was necessary to expel the student under the prevailing conditions. According to the social mores of the period, boys and girls had to
be strictly separated. It was necessary to maintain the paternal
family system and produce strong soldiers at that time." Surely
one of the motives behind Munakata's lifelong study of education
was the example of his father.

It is somewhat ironic that both father and son experienced
times of war. The father lived through the Sino-Japanese and
Russo-Japanese wars. The son graduated from Tokyo Imperial University in 1931, at the beginning of a new active phase
of Japanese imperialism marked by the Manchurian Incident.
Even while he was a university student, the winds of oppression
were blowing around young Munakata as the Special Security
Police stepped up their activities against left-wing student organizations. For example, in 1928, the Tokyo Imperial University
Shinjinkai, an organization of students whose aim was to promote
socialism, was dissolved by order of the police. Many students
at several universities, along with a number of professors, were
arrested for opposing war. The dark clouds of aggression were
forming on the horizon.

Throughout the period prior to 1941, Munakata was deeply
involved in protest movements. For example, in 1937, when the
Japanese invasion of mainland China was under way, he organized the Society for the Study of Educational Science. The
statement of purpose of the organization stated that

the study of education has fallen far behind the needs of
society. Indeed the social function of the school has not been
fulfilled. We must recognize that the reform of the school
is not simply a problem of pedagogy but a social prob-

lem. In order to reform society, we must reform our system of education. For that purpose, we hereby organize this Society which aims at the scientific reconstruction of education.

The group took its initial stance against militaristic education, which was based on the Imperial Rescript on Education promulgated in 1890. In his book *My Declaration of Education* [*Watakushi no Kyoiku Sengen*], published immediately after the war, Munakata wrote that

> our group was in reality a resistance movement based on humanism and realism contrary to the dogmatic system of education of the day. Some of the teachers from the Tsuzurikata Kyoiku Undo (Educational Movement Through Children's Writings) took part in our activities. I was struck with admiration for the classroom teachers who joined our struggles, which motivated me to devote my studies to the actual problems of education. That was the reason why I decided to resign from the University of Tokyo and its "ivory-tower" environment.
>
> Shortly afterward, the activities of the Society's study circles were suppressed by the authorities. It was obvious that they could not be tolerated by the militarists in power, who were moving toward all-out war in the Pacific. At any rate, through my activities in this movement I proved to myself that I could make a contribution in the historical struggle to try and solve the social problems of our country. I express my eternal gratitude to my colleagues in this movement.

Professor Munakata's postwar activities in promoting the ideals of democratic education clearly had their roots in his prewar experiences. His participation in similar movements prior to the war were pursued after he took up his new position on the faculty of Hosei University. Looking back on that eventful period in his life, he wrote that

> I never once felt like influencing others through my position at the University of Tokyo. If I had one good trait, it was

that I indulged myself at times by thinking of myself as a king without a crown.

During the war I convinced myself that it was sufficient to outwardly show loyalty to the Emperor. I really didn't want to be a rebel. I wished to die an honorable death. I didn't want youth to die alone.

I was subsequently able to find a part-time position in the Japanese Association of Industry, which took me to plants producing military aircraft—targets of aerial attacks. I concluded that the enemy forces would probably land at Kashima Bay, so I tried to find a position nearby. I had become desperate and distraught.

I was then appointed director of the Kokumin Seikatsu Gakuin, a type of welfare school for girls under the association's supervision. I tried to set a good example for the girls as a loyal subject. I was also afraid of being arrested because of my previous activities. I worried that my students would be thrown into confusion if I were taken away by the authorities. To be a teacher was a difficult burden for me.

One can readily see why I felt such enthusiasm for the slogan the Japan Teachers' Union used after the war: "Never send our children into battle again." Those sentiments meant a great deal to me as a result of my previous experiences. Indeed, when I read the Report of the United States Education Mission to Japan in 1946, I was full of gratitude. I felt that I had finally been liberated.

The academic achievements of Professor Munakata have extended thus from the prewar to the postwar periods. For example, in 1937, in one of his earlier articles, entitled "The Scientific Study of Pedagogy" (*"Kyoiku no Kagakuteki Kenkyuho to Sono Mondai"*), he revealed his approach to the discipline of education. Pedagogy, he concluded,

has not reached a level of maturity in the sense that it has become a study for its own sake. The problems of education in the real world of the classroom teacher are not studied. Rather, the philosophical theories of education have become the central focus of pedagogical research.

The study of education has strayed far from the school itself. It has become based on the philosophical analyses of certain theoretical scholars. This makes it virtually impossible to carefully accumulate a body of knowledge based on the actual problems facing the school into the formation of the scientific study of pedagogy. How can these problems ever be solved?

One can see that Professor Munakata's approach to the study of education was intimately related to the life of the child and the teacher in school. He was, as mentioned previously, deeply impressed and influenced by the classroom teachers who had participated in the prewar movements against militaristic education. As a result, he wrote another article, "An Inquiry into the Science of Education" ("*Kyoiku Kagaku Ron no Kento*"), in which he said that "the most fundamental issue facing our discipline is the relationship between theory and practice." He argued that the developing theory must be founded on reality, otherwise it is not a scientific method: "The problems we should be attempting to solve come from the classroom. The direction of our scientific study should be decided by the practical necessities of the school itself."

Thus, when Japan went down to defeat in World War II, it was a natural consequence that Professor Munakata would put his heart and soul into the postwar movement to "reform society through education." Pedagogy, the study of educational problems facing the nation, became his focus: "Pedagogy as a discipline is not the urgent matter facing us. Renewal and reform of Japanese education is a matter of life or death for the nation itself."

As the late Professor Kaigo of the University of Tokyo said in his memorial address, Munakata is regarded as an outstanding leader in the field of education who pioneered in the scientific study of educational administration. Consequently there have been many books, papers, and articles written about him and his academic contributions. The major treatise that compiles his writings on educational administration is *Kyōiku Gyōseigaku Josetsu* (*An Introduction to Educational Administration*), revised in 1965. From that publication and another, "The Fundamental

Law of Education," published in 1966, we can summarize his thinking.

Article X of the Fundamental Law of Education begins with the following provision under the heading "School Administration": "Education shall not be subject to improper control, but it shall be directly responsible to the whole people. . . . School administration shall, on the basis of this realization, aim at the adjustment and establishment of the various conditions required for the pursuit of education."

Munakata explained that the basic spirit underlying this law originated from the report of the United States Education Mission to Japan expressed in the preamble of the law:

> Having established the Constitution of Japan, we have shown our resolution to contribute to the peace of the world and welfare of humanity by building a democratic and cultural state. The realization of this ideal shall depend fundamentally on the power of education. We shall esteem individual dignity and endeavor to bring up people who love truth and peace, while education which aims at the creation of culture, general and rich in individuality, shall be spread far and wide. We hereby enact this Law, in accordance with the spirit of the Constitution of Japan, with a view to clarify the aim of education and establishing the foundation of education for a new Japan.

Munakata then argued that Article X of the Fundamental Law of Education had been mutilated by the 1956 Law for the Organization and Management of Local Educational Administration. The specific provision of the new law that is the focus of his criticism concerns the revision of the school-board system. From the beginning of the new school boards in 1948, the members were chosen through local elections. From 1956 they were selected by the local mayor or prefectural governor. Munakata concluded that the three basic principles of school administration after the war—democracy, decentralization, and local autonomy—were severely undermined by the new law, which drastically altered the locally elected lay principle of the original school-board law.

In his unending struggle against "improper control of education by the government," Munakata played a very active role in various court cases. He testified on behalf of the defendants in a number of landmark cases, often on behalf of members of the Japan Teachers' Union. His basic position can be summarized from the testimony.

The basis of his thinking rests on the interpretation of the critical phrase *improper control* imbedded in the Fundamental Law of Education. According to Munakata, it must be strictly defined. For example, a financial group, a labor union, or a specific political party, would clearly fall within the purview of "improper control" if they attempted to gain power over the schools. However, where the misunderstanding of this critical phrase takes place is in its relationship to the government or state power itself. The Fundamental Law of Education severely restricts the government from improperly controlling the school through its power.

The original intention of the Report of the United States Education Mission to Japan was to curtail the power of the state over education, and that is the intent of the Fundamental Law of Education which grew out of the Mission's report. More specifically, the state has no right to set the curriculum or approve the textbooks, according to Munakata's interpretation of the law, in contrast to the actual practice beginning with the 1956 Law for the Organization and Management of Local Educational Administration. The state itself has thus exerted "improper control" over school affairs.

From this theoretical interpretation of the law, Munakata appealed to teachers not to permit the central governmental authorities to intervene in management of their classroom. The role of the Ministry of Education in local school affairs was intended purely as an advisory one. Any action that went beyond that constituted an infringement of local autonomy and the role and responsibility of the teacher in local school affairs. Professor Munakata thus became perhaps the central figure in developing a scientific theory of school administration in the massive postwar movement against the power of the state in local school affairs. This should be recognized as perhaps his most outstanding contribution to the field of education.

The introduction by the government of a system of local school management also incurred the wrath of Munakata. Principal-ships and vice-principalships were declared administrative positions. Consequently they were not allowed to be members of the Japan Teachers' Union, forcing many of them to withdraw from membership upon enforcement. In addition, a system of department heads and various other semi-administrative positions was established with various financial inducements paid for assuming the extra duties. At the bottom of the structure stood the regular classroom teacher.

Munakata branded the government's theory of school administration the "theory of a stratified school." He charged that the government merely established mechanically a theory of business administration based on the American industrial world. The school was viewed in the same perspective as a manufacturing company with a stratified organization of employees from the executives to the managers down to the workers on the shop floor. When applied to the school, the principal and vice-principal were viewed as the executives, the department heads as the managers, and the teachers as the shop-floor workers.

The daily operation of the school was likewise conducted from the perspective of a company. Each plan, be it the daily teaching plan or the weekly or monthly plan of studies, was drawn up based on guidelines set by the government. The managers and executives—that is, the department heads and the principal—reviewed the plans to make certain they followed the guidelines sent down from above. All decisions affecting the school were made by the managers and executives. The only course for the classroom teacher was to follow the orders from above. The rights of teachers were ignored in the process—and this, Munakata scoffed, was called the "modern management of the curriculum" by the government.

To Munakata, this theory of management failed to recognize that the school has a unique character different from that of a manufacturing firm. A company must distinguish the various levels of responsibility among its employees. However, in a local school, every teacher except the principal has the responsibility for teaching his classes. There can be no distinction among the teachers according to age, sex, or experience. Even the head teacher has a teaching responsibility equal to that of the others.

Therefore, head teachers should be elected from among the teachers on a rotating basis.

It is an indispensable feature of every school that all members of the staff except the principal be responsible for teaching. The role of school management is to raise the morale of the teachers so that each one will be inspired to teach to the best of his or her ability with a seriousness of purpose. To rob teachers of their passion for teaching by rendering them robots following blindly the guidelines set down by the government and enforced by a set of local school officials destroys the real purpose of education and leads the nation into decay.

Up to now we have seen Munakata primarily as an educator in the pursuit of a democratic school system. But his activities extended beyond the school and even beyond the borders of Japan itself as his pacifistic beliefs motivated him to act on international matters. In 1968, the Japanese Committee for the Investigation of War Crimes in Vietnam was set up by a group of intellectuals. It was inspired by the International Court of War Crimes in Vietnam proposed by Bertrand Russell. Munakata took the lead in setting up the Japanese committee, serving as the chairman of the steering committee for its widely publicized activities.

Munakata explained why he became involved in this international affair, though "only a mere scholar on education." By that time he felt that Japanese education was being devastated by the consuming emphasis on examination preparation and the increasingly competitive nature of the school. For example, the enforcement of the Teachers' Efficiency Rating System in Ehime Prefecture, against the strong opposition of the teachers' union, and the use of the Nationwide Scholastic Achievement Test denied the dignity of both the teacher and the student. The government's textbook authorization system, then being challenged in the courts in the famous cases in which historian Ienaga Saburo sued the government for compelling him to revise his history text before receiving authorization, was another step in a dangerous direction.

The direction in which the government was heading, in the mind of Munakata, was clearly toward a rebirth of militarism. The military links between Japan and America, already joined by a military alliance, were further strengthened during the Vietnam War. America, Japan's military ally, had been committing atrocities in Vietnam. The war in Vietnam and the American role in it had to be denounced. It could have a long-range effect on Japanese society and the school.

Munakata's role in the international movement against the Vietnam War, as well as the many other activities of this great educator from Japan during both the prewar and postwar periods, were summed up in his final brief writing. Two weeks before he passed away, he wrote a simple message to be read at the 1970 annual conference of the Japan Teachers' Union. It not only summarizes in a brief passage his basic convictions, it turned out to be his last and most fitting testimony: "To all of you who have gathered at this convention, I want to express my resolution to struggle together with you to the end for peace and democracy."

Munakata's contributions to Japanese education are as vital and alive today as they were when he made them. For example, in the mid-1980s, the Japanese government under the behest of the prime minister launched a major investigation into the needs of Japanese education for the twenty-first century in order to carry out "sweeping reforms" of the present system. A special council made up of representatives from different sectors of the society was appointed by the government to carry out the study.

One of the important issues referred to so frequently by council members in their deliberations concerns the provisions of the Fundamental Law of Education. This is significant because Munakata developed his theoretical position against governmental interference in local education based on an interpretation of the meaning and intent of the provisions of the Fundamental Law of Education. The controversy that engulfed his life and consumed his energies has been resurrected by this council. His interpretation is as relevant today as it was during his lifetime.

One member of the council, a vice president of Zen Nihon Rodo Sodomei (the Japan Federation of Labor), presented the opinion that the aim of education, as expressed in the Fundamental Law, to develop the full personality of the individual is difficult to clearly interpret and understand. To certain members of the council, personality independent of nationality and the state does not exist. The Fundamental Law should be reconsidered from the point of view of what kind of personality we should be developing as a nation. Another member from the business community claimed that the Fundamental Law implied the development of a religious sentiment, a patriotic sentiment, and the respect for tradition. Many other similar opinions were expressed.

There are those who fear that the reform of education in the 1980s may be headed in a direction too similar to that of the prewar era, when the Imperial Rescript of Education was the dominating influence on Japanese education. It would be advisable to look once again at Munakata's writings on this very issue, which is once again before the nation. In his well-known writings on the Fundamental Law of Education, he argued that pedagogy and the Fundamental Law of Education are intricately related:

> When education loses its independence, teachers are corrupted by the government. When teachers become corrupt, education deteriorates. The deterioration of education destroys the humanity of children. We cannot expect the dignity of the individual to be recognized, according to the Fundamental Law, under the present system of education, much less the respect for academic freedom and freedom of speech under the textbook approval system carried out with government control. Under these alarming conditions, it cannot be repeated too often that the spirit of the Fundamental Law of Education must be reconfirmed again and again.

There is a growing fear once again that the spirit of the Fundamental Law of Education is being eroded in the current investigation into the reforms of education. Consequently many of the teachers and scholars who were deeply influenced by Munakata are organizing a movement against the government's attempts to reform education. Rather, these concerned people are endeavoring to develop principles for the reform of education based on the spirit of the Constitution and the Fundamental Law of Education through a broadly based nationwide campaign. If Munakata were alive today, he would surely be in the forefront of this movement.

The chairman of the Japan Teachers' Union demonstrated that the influence of Munakata remains virtually as strong in the mid-1980s as it was during his lifetime:

The council appointed by the government to study the problems of education is deliberating on the issues with little reference to the actual problems of the school and the classroom. We are apprehensive about our children's future and the future of Japanese education in the twenty-first century. Accordingly we must reconfirm our support of the Fundamental Law of Education as Professor Munakata advocated to the very end. We must always remember his belief in the spirit of the Fundamental Law of Education as a warning against the present trends in Japanese education.

The Life of Munakata Seiya

1908	Born in Tokyo.
1931	Graduated from the Faculty of Humanities, Tokyo Imperial University.
1932	Named Assistant in the Faculty of Humanities, Tokyo Imperial University.
1939 -1946	Lectured at Toyo University, St. Paul's University and Kanazawa University; Professor at Hosei University; Director of Kokumin Seikatsu Gakuin (Institute for People's Livelihood); Director of Nihon Shuppan Kai (Japan Press Society); and Secretary of the Dai Nippon Kyoiku Kai (All-Japan Education Society).
1948	Published *The Reconstruction of Education*.
1949	Named Professor in the Faculty of Education, University of Tokyo.
1950	Published *The Law of Educational Research*.
1951	Served as advisor to the Japan Teachers' Union's First National Teachers' Conference for the Study of Education.
1952	Named Director of the Nihon Kyoiku Gakkai (Japan

Society for the Study of Education).

1954 Published *Introduction to Educational Administration.*

1955 Appointed Dean of the Faculty of Education, University of Tokyo.

1960 Named a member of the Science Council of Japan.

1961 Published *Educational and Educational Policy.*

1966 Published *The Fundamental Law of Education* and *The Reconstruction of Education.*

1967 Published *The Educational Rights of the People and Teachers.*

1969 Retired from the University of Tokyo.

1970 Died at age 62.

About the Author

Muneaki Mochizuki was born in 1922 in Yamanashi Prefecture, and graduated in 1946 from Meiji Gakuin University. In 1947 he joined the staff of *Shukan Kyoiku Shimbun* (The Education Weekly), and in 1949 he joined the staff of the Japan Teachers' Union as its Historian. His publications (in Japanese) include *The Educational Labor Movement* (1970), *The Thirty-Year History of the Japan Teachers' Union* (1977), and *Women Teachers in Japan.*

Index

GALLAUDET UNIVERSITY

3 2884 000 007 376

370.952 T4 1989   038581